Study Guide for Decoding The Merchant of Venice

With Typical Questions and Answers

Steven Smith

Sherwood Press

CONTENTS

— ◆ —

How to use this guide

This analysis of William Shakespeare's "Merchant of Venice" intends to offer a study guide to readers who need a more in-depth view of the story.

This book is divided into questions, so the answers appear in a short essay style and may include repeated information. The questions are typical of what a high school student may experience.

I want to think all important questions have been either directly or indirectly answered. However, if you, the reader, feel something is missing, please reach out to me, and I will add it!

Happy studying!

Steven Smith

stevensmithvo@gmail.com

www.classicbooksexplained.com

— • —

Unveiling the Mysteries

Unveiling the Mysteries is a study guide series to help readers understand and enjoy commonly-read English masterpieces.

Available exclusively on Amazon, look for the Classic Books Explained series by Steven Smith

As of the writing of this novel, here are the books in the series;

1. Study Guide: Unveiling the Mysteries of Merchant of Venice: With Typical Questions and Answers

2. Study Guide: Unveiling the Mysteries of Othello: With Typical Questions and Answers

3. Study Guide: Unveiling the Mysteries of Midsummer Night's Dream: With Typical Questions and Answers

4. Study Guide: Unveiling the Mysteries of Julius Caesar: With Typical Questions and Answers

5. Study Guide: Unveiling the Mysteries of The Scarlet Letter: With Typical Questions and Answers

6. Study guide: Unveiling the Mysteries of Wuthering Heights: With Typical Questions and Answers

7. Study Guide: Unveiling the Mysteries of The Catcher in the Rye:

WHAT IS THE HISTORICAL BACKGROUND TO WILLIAM SHAKESPEARE'S MERCHANT OF VENICE?

"Merchant of Venice" is one of William Shakespeare's most famous plays, first believed to have been performed around 1596-1597. The play, set in Venice, Italy, is a complex blend of romance, comedy, and dramatic elements and deals with themes like mercy, justice, and the relationship between law and morality.

The period in which the play was written, the late 16th and early 17th century, is called the Elizabethan Era. This time is characterized by England's relative stability and prosperity under Queen Elizabeth I. London, where Shakespeare was based, had become a vibrant center of commerce and culture. This period was also the height of the English Renaissance, with a flourishing of arts, literature, and theater.

However, the time was also marked by religious conflict and tension, both within England and between England and other countries. England was officially Protestant under Elizabeth I, following the Reformation, and there was a significant amount of prejudice and suspicion towards Catholics. Additionally, there was intense discrimination against Jewish people, who had been expelled from England in 1290 and were often the subject of negative stereotypes and depictions, as can be seen in the character of Shylock in "Merchant of Venice".

The setting of the play, Venice, was a significant global trading center during this period. It was known for its wealth, cultural richness, and for its democratic governance compared to many other European states which were ruled by monarchs. Venice was also known for being a city where people of different religions and cultures, including Jews, interacted, although there were restrictions and Jews lived in areas known as ghettos.

In "Merchant of Venice", Shakespeare seems to have taken inspiration from Italian tales and contemporary English literature. One source might have been "Il Pecorone" (The Simpleton), a collection of stories by Giovanni Fiorentino, which includes a tale that has parallels to the play. There is also a similar story in "Gesta Romanorum", a Latin collection of anecdotes and tales.

The attitudes towards Jews reflected in "Merchant of Venice", particularly in the character of Shylock, have been the subject of much analysis and controversy. Shylock is portrayed as a moneylender who demands a "pound of flesh" as repayment for a loan, a portrayal which is seen as reinforcing negative stereotypes about Jews. Some argue that the play reflects the anti-Semitic attitudes of the time, while others suggest that it is more complex and that Shakespeare was critiquing such attitudes. This question continues to be debated among scholars and theatre practitioners.

Lastly, the legal and economic themes in the play reflect issues of the time, such as the role of moneylending and the balance of mercy and justice in law, reflecting the transformations that were happening in the English society and economy.

WHAT KIND OF PLAY IS THIS

"The Merchant of Venice" is technically classified as a comedy in the canon of Shakespeare's works, but this designation primarily refers to the structure of the play and its ending rather than its tone or content. Comedies in Shakespeare's time were plays that ended in marriage rather than death, which differentiates them from tragedies. In "The Merchant of Venice," there are multiple marriages—between Portia and Bassanio, and between Lorenzo and Jessica, for instance—which signifies a comedic conclusion.

However, modern audiences often find the categorization of "The Merchant of Venice" as a comedy unsettling due to the tragic elements and heavy themes it contains. Shylock's downfall and the anti-Semitic treatment he endures throughout the play infuse the narrative with a decidedly tragic tone. His famous monologue ("Hath not a Jew eyes?") conveys profound emotional suffering, making him a character who evokes empathy and sadness.

The play also delves into issues such as religious intolerance, revenge, and mercy, which are themes often associated with tragedies.

Given these complexities, some scholars and critics refer to "The Merchant of Venice" as a 'problem play'. The term 'problem play' is used to describe Shakespeare's plays that do not fit neatly into the traditional classification of tragedy or comedy. These plays, which also include "Measure for Measure" and "All's Well That Ends Well," are characterized by their blending of comedic and tragic elements, and their exploration of complex moral and social issues.

So, while "The Merchant of Venice" is technically a comedy based on its structure and ending, it contains elements of tragedy and problem plays, making it a complex and multifaceted work that defies easy classification.

—·—

WHY DO STUDENTS STUDY MERCHANT OF VENICE

"The Merchant of Venice" is a significant work in the Western literary canon, and studying it can offer students several educational benefits:

1. **Literary Merit**: As one of Shakespeare's plays, "The Merchant of Venice" has high literary quality. It's filled with rich language, complex characters, dramatic tension, and thoughtful themes. Studying the play can help students develop skills in analyzing text, understanding plot and character development, interpreting symbolic language and imagery, and appreciating the aesthetic qualities of literature.

2. **Understanding Historical and Cultural Context**: The play provides insights into the Elizabethan era, including attitudes toward money, law, religion, and societal hierarchy. It also gives a glimpse into the historical relationships between Christians and Jews and the stereotypes and biases that existed during Shakespeare's time. This can facilitate discussions about historical context, cultural differences, and the evolution of societal norms and values.

3. **Exploration of Themes**: The play delves into universal themes such as love, justice, mercy, prejudice, and the nature of good and evil. These themes resonate even today and can spark meaningful class discussions and personal reflections.

4. **Understanding and Appreciating Shakespeare**: Shakespeare's works have had a profound influence on English literature and language. Studying his plays is a traditional part of many high school curricula and helps students appreciate his contributions. This familiarity can also help students understand references to Shakespeare that they may encounter in other texts, in popular culture, or in academic settings.

5. **Critical Thinking and Empathy**: Studying "The Merchant of Venice" can encourage critical thinking about challenging issues. For instance, the character of Shylock — a Jewish moneylender who is both a villain and a victim — can spark discussions about bias, discrimination, and empathy. Analyzing a complex character like Shylock can help students develop empathy and nuanced thinking.

6. **Engagement with Controversial Issues**: The play's depiction of anti-Semitism provides an opportunity to engage with issues of discrimination and prejudice. Teachers can use it as a starting point to discuss historical and contemporary forms of bias and bigotry, helping students to reflect on these issues in a safe and structured environment.

While "The Merchant of Venice" can be challenging, particularly because of its archaic language and controversial themes, it can also provide a rewarding educational experience when taught with sensitivity and contextual understanding.

LITERARY MERITS

William Shakespeare's "The Merchant of Venice" is a seminal work of English literature that exhibits a wealth of literary merits. Its multifaceted exploration of universal themes, its richly conceived characters, the eloquence and versatility of its language, and its deft balance of comedy, romance, and tragedy attest to its stature as a masterwork of the Elizabethan era.

The brilliance of the play rests in part on its examination of enduring themes. The central theme of justice versus mercy, for instance, comes to the fore in the famous courtroom scene. Portia's entreaty to Shylock – "The quality of mercy is not strained... It blesseth him that gives, and him that takes" (Act 4, Scene 1) – is a powerful meditation on the nobility of forgiveness over strict adherence to law. This dialogue not only sparks philosophical rumination on the nature of mercy and justice but is emblematic of Shakespeare's ability to transform complex ideas into poetic language.

The theme of appearance versus reality is also skillfully woven throughout the play. Jessica, Shylock's daughter, disguises herself as a boy to elope with Lorenzo, thus challenging societal norms and expectations. Portia and Nerissa also disguise themselves as men in the courtroom scene, leading to delightful comedic moments and profound revelations about gender and power. This subversion of appearances underscores the idea that identity is multifaceted and mutable.

The play's characters are another testament to its literary merit. Each character is complex and dynamic, revealing multiple facets of their personality as the narrative unfolds. Shylock, for instance, is not a mere villain but a character whose hostility emerges from a background of discrimination and prejudice. His poignant soliloquy, "Hath not a Jew eyes? Hath not a Jew hands, organs, dimensions, senses, affections, passions?" (Act 3, Scene 1), reveals his humanity, challenging the audience's perception and fostering empathy.

Portia, another standout character, exemplifies intelligence, wit, and grace. While she is bound by her father's will in the casket lottery, she uses her intelligence to steer Bassanio towards the correct choice. Her cunning is also displayed in the trial scene where, disguised as Balthazar, she manipulately interprets the law to save Antonio, demonstrating a woman's agency in a male-dominated society.

The language of "The Merchant of Venice" is a masterclass in Elizabethan verse, reflecting Shakespeare's unparalleled dexterity with words. His use of diverse literary devices like metaphors, similes, puns, and irony enriches the text, enhancing its evocative power and emotional resonance. For example, Antonio's opening lines, "In sooth, I know not why I am so sad" (Act 1, Scene 1), immediately set a somber tone, while Portia's "The quality of mercy is not strained" speech employs vivid metaphors to present an elegant argument for compassion.

The play's tonal versatility, straddling comedy, romance, and tragedy, adds to its literary merit. The comedic elements often serve to offset the darker themes and events, such as the bond of the "pound of flesh," maintaining a delicate balance that keeps the audience engaged. The romantic subplot involving Portia and Bassanio adds a softer dimension, making the play a complex blend of genres.

In conclusion, "The Merchant of Venice," with its nuanced exploration of universal themes, its complex characters who grapple with moral dilemmas, its rich and versatile language, and its adroit blend of comedy, romance, and tragedy, holds an unassailable position in the realm of world literature. The play is a testament to Shakespeare's extraordinary ability to delve into the depths of the human condition, and its literary merits continue to captivate, enlighten, and inspire students, scholars, and audiences alike.

HISTORICAL AND CULTURAL CONTEXTS

"The Merchant of Venice" is one of William Shakespeare's most renowned plays, and to understand it fully, we must look closely at the historical and cultural contexts in which it was written and set.

The play was likely written between 1596 and 1599, during the reign of Queen Elizabeth I, a period characterized by relative political stability and growth. It was a time of religious tension between Protestants and Catholics following the English Reformation, marked by profound anti-Semitic sentiments, as Jews had been expelled from England in the late 13th century and negative stereotypes pervaded. However, it's essential to note that this prejudice wasn't limited to England but was widespread throughout Europe, affecting all aspects of Jewish life, including where they could live and work.

Shakespeare set "The Merchant of Venice" in the Italian city of Venice, one of the wealthiest and most powerful city-states during the Renaissance. Known for its multiculturalism, Venice was a global trade center where people of different religions and cultures, including Jews, co-existed—though not without discrimination.

Venice was a republic known for its legalistic approach to governance and its comprehensive judicial system. This historical fact is vital to understand the letter-of-the-law insistence of Shylock, the Jewish moneylender, on his contract with Antonio, the merchant. Shylock's insistence on a "pound of flesh" (Act 1, Scene 3) is not mere cruel vengeance, but the strict adherence to legal rights which Venice, as a city, was known for.

Although there were Jewish communities in Venice, they were required to live in areas known as ghettos. The term 'ghetto' originated in Venice, referring to the area where Jews were compelled to live. Despite such enforced segregation, the city's economy relied heavily on the Jewish community's financial activities, especially money lending. This fact highlights the societal paradox in the play, where Shylock is both needed and scorned.

Shakespeare's depiction of Shylock is not a flattering one, in line with the anti-Semitic attitudes of the time. However, the playwright also challenges these prejudices by humanizing Shylock in his famous speech in Act 3, Scene 1, where he argues for his humanity - "Hath not a Jew eyes? Hath not a Jew hands, organs, dimensions, senses, affections, passions?" Here, Shakespeare grants Shylock a voice to challenge the discrimination he faces, revealing the playwright's skill in adding layers of complexity to his characters.

The play's portrayal of women and marriage is also reflective of the cultural norms of the Elizabethan era. Women in Shakespeare's time were largely regarded as property, to be given away in marriage along with a dowry. This cultural reality is reflected in the subplot of the caskets, where Portia's suitors must choose between three caskets to win her hand. Portia's predicament, her lack of agency in choosing her husband, highlights the patriarchal norms of the time.

Yet, Shakespeare's Portia is not a docile character but a clever, resourceful woman who eventually turns the tide of the play. This depiction of women subtly challenges the societal norms. By portraying a strong, intelligent female character who outwits men, saves Antonio, and controls her destiny, Shakespeare seems to be undermining the patriarchal society's constraints.

Religious tensions in "The Merchant of Venice" between Christians and Jews are not merely historical reflections; they echo the broader Elizabethan societal tensions between Protestants and Catholics. As such, the conflict can be seen as an allegorical exploration of religious discrimination and intolerance prevalent in Elizabethan England.

The economic activities in the play, such as maritime commerce and money lending, reflect the real economic transformation happening in England during the Elizabethan era. Shakespeare's England was moving from a feudal economy to a more market-based system, where cash transactions became more common. This shift is apparent in the play, where business ventures and financial dealings form the plot's backbone.

In conclusion, "The Merchant of Venice" is deeply rooted in the cultural and historical contexts of its time. To comprehend its themes, characters, and conflicts, we must appreciate its reflections of Venice's multicultural atmosphere, the economic realities of the time, Elizabethan norms regarding gender and marriage, and the societal and religious tensions of the era. It is in this context that Shakespeare's play comes alive, offering us a rich, nuanced, and deeply human exploration of universal themes such as justice, mercy, love, prejudice, and the multifaceted nature of humanity. The play's enduring relevance and power lie in its capacity to resonate with audiences across cultures and eras, compelling us to reflect on our prejudices and societal norms.

— • —

THEMES

"The Merchant of Venice," one of William Shakespeare's most complex and multi-layered plays, explores a plethora of themes, each intricate and deeply ingrained within the story's fabric. Themes such as mercy versus justice, love and friendship, appearance versus reality, prejudice, and the interplay of religion and law resonate with audiences across centuries.

One of the central themes of "The Merchant of Venice" is the conflict between mercy and justice, predominantly illustrated in the courtroom scene in Act 4. Shylock demands "justice," insisting on his legal right to claim a pound of Antonio's flesh as repayment for his defaulted loan. In stark contrast, Portia pleads for mercy, delivering one of the most famous speeches in the play – "The quality of mercy is not strained... It blesseth him that gives, and him that takes" (Act 4, Scene 1). This eloquent plea contrasts the harshness of justice without compassion. Portia's argument suggests that mercy, a divine attribute, humanizes the law and makes society more harmonious and humane.

The theme of love and friendship is another crucial thread running through the play. The close friendship between Antonio and Bassanio sets the story in motion, as Antonio's willingness to risk his life to help his friend emphasizes the deep bond between them. In parallel, romantic love is explored through various relationships. Portia and Bassanio's love story is central, with their courtship framed within the casket challenge set by Portia's late father. This subplot showcases the various forms love can take – including the dutiful love of a daughter (Portia adhering to her father's will), the love between friends (Bassanio seeking Antonio's help to woo Portia), and the romantic love between Portia and Bassanio.

The theme of appearance versus reality is manifest throughout the play, which abounds in disguises and deceptions. Portia and Nerissa's disguises as a lawyer and his clerk in the trial scene exemplify this theme. Their successful deception not only saves Antonio's life but also enables them to test their respective husbands' fidelity by asking for their rings as a fee, challenging the audience's understanding of gender roles and fidelity. Shylock, too, is not what he initially appears to be. Although portrayed as a villain, his eloquent speech in Act 3, Scene 1 reveals his humanity and the pain caused by Christian intolerance, showing the disparity between his outward label as a villain and his inner emotional landscape.

Prejudice, particularly religious prejudice, is a significant theme in "The Merchant of Venice." Shakespeare vividly illustrates the religious and racial tensions of his time, notably through the character of Shylock. The play underscores the discrimination and ostracism faced by Jews through Shylock's experiences. In his poignant "Hath not a Jew eyes?" speech (Act 3, Scene 1), Shylock exposes the hypocrisy and cruelty of the Christian characters, encouraging empathy and understanding from the audience.

Interestingly, the character of Shylock also allows the play to explore the tension between religious law and secular law. This tension becomes evident when Shylock, following Jewish law and customs, lends money to Antonio, expecting interest – a practice forbidden in Christian law. The final courtroom scene is a battleground of these differing laws, with Shylock insisting on the enforcement of a secular contract, while Portia appeals to Christian principles of mercy to circumvent its fatal consequence.

The theme of material wealth versus human value threads its way through the narrative. Bassanio seeks Portia not only for her virtues but also her wealth, while Antonio risks his life for Bassanio's cause. Shylock's insistence on a pound of flesh as repayment represents the extreme commodification of human life, while Portia's "quality of mercy" speech promotes the principle of human value over material wealth. The conflict between these opposing values is encapsulated in the three casket challenge, where choosing lead (symbolizing inner worth) over gold and silver (symbolizing external wealth) wins Portia's hand.

In conclusion, the exploration of themes such as mercy versus justice, love and friendship, appearance versus reality, prejudice, the interplay of religious and secular law, and the conflict between material wealth and human value makes "The Merchant of Venice" a rich and resonant play. Shakespeare's masterful handling of these themes imbues the narrative with depth and complexity, engaging the audience's intellect and emotions. The play's enduring relevance lies in its ability to provoke reflection on these timeless themes, challenging our values and assumptions and, in turn, enriching our understanding of the human condition.

Understanding and Appreciation of Shakespeare

Understanding and appreciating Shakespeare's "The Merchant of Venice" is a multi-layered journey that not only involves dissecting the themes, language, characters, and narrative structure of the play but also comprehending its historical context and enduring cultural relevance. This exploration reveals Shakespeare's genius in dramatizing complex human experiences, his profound understanding of societal norms and prejudices, and his extraordinary gift for language.

"The Merchant of Venice" is a shining example of Shakespeare's mastery of plot construction. The play seamlessly interweaves two distinct plot lines: Antonio and Shylock's bond story and the romantic courtship between Portia and Bassanio. Despite their apparent difference in tone and content, these storylines converge in the courtroom scene, demonstrating Shakespeare's unparalleled skill in creating a cohesive and compelling narrative.

Shakespeare's portrayal of complex, three-dimensional characters is another aspect of his genius. Each character in "The Merchant of Venice," whether major or minor, is nuanced and multi-faceted. Shylock, one of the most memorable characters, is neither a straightforward villain nor a tragic hero. Despite his vengeful stance, audiences can empathize with his plight as a marginalized and persecuted individual. His famous speech, "Hath not a Jew eyes?" (Act 3, Scene 1), underscores his humanity and the prejudice he faces. Such character depth prompts audiences to challenge their preconceived notions, demonstrating Shakespeare's keen insight into the human condition.

The women characters, particularly Portia, are remarkably well-crafted and progressive for their time. Despite being subjected to patriarchal norms, Portia manipulates the situation to her advantage, ultimately outwitting the men and saving Antonio. This nuanced portrayal of women hints at Shakespeare's progressive attitude towards gender roles and his understanding of women's intellectual capacity and agency, enhancing our appreciation of his vision and craftsmanship.

Shakespeare's mastery of language is evident in the play's varied and emotive dialogues. The text's sheer linguistic richness, ranging from the eloquent rhetoric in Portia's "quality of mercy" speech (Act 4, Scene 1) to the raw emotion in Shylock's "Hath not a Jew eyes?" speech, reflects Shakespeare's unique ability to encapsulate profound ideas in beautiful and compelling language. His use of diverse literary devices such as metaphors, similes, and dramatic irony adds depth and layers of meaning to the text, making his works a source of continual exploration and discovery.

Shakespeare's treatment of themes such as mercy versus justice, love and friendship, prejudice, and appearance versus reality reveals his deep understanding of societal norms and human nature. His exploration of these themes invites audiences to reflect on their values, attitudes, and behaviors, making the play relevant across different cultural and historical contexts. The way he exposes and challenges societal prejudices and hypocrisies, particularly through the character of Shylock, testifies to his progressive outlook and critical social commentary.

An appreciation of "The Merchant of Venice" must also involve understanding its historical and cultural context. The play reflects the religious and racial tensions of Shakespeare's time, providing insight into Elizabethan societal norms and attitudes. Recognizing this historical backdrop enables a deeper understanding of the characters' motivations and the themes explored in the play. However, the play's enduring relevance also lies in its ability to resonate with contemporary issues such as racial discrimination, religious intolerance, and gender roles, demonstrating the universality of Shakespeare's works.

Finally, appreciating "The Merchant of Venice" entails recognizing its multifaceted nature. The play straddles various genres, combining elements of comedy, romance, and tragedy. Its ability to oscillate between moments of high tension and light-hearted humor, between romantic charm and tragic intensity, highlights Shakespeare's versatility as a playwright.

In conclusion, understanding and appreciating "The Merchant of Venice" involves exploring its rich narrative, complex characters, masterful language, profound themes, historical context, and genre-blending nature. This journey into the play reveals Shakespeare's genius as a storyteller, his deep understanding of human nature and societal norms, and his timeless relevance. His ability to engage, challenge, and move audiences centuries after his death testifies to his enduring legacy and his unparalleled position in the realm of world literature.

CRITICAL THINKING AND EMPATHY

Studying "The Merchant of Venice" offers an invaluable opportunity for students to develop critical thinking skills and empathy, two crucial components in understanding literature and human experience.

Critical thinking involves questioning assumptions, analyzing information, and formulating independent judgments. In "The Merchant of Venice," Shakespeare presents complex situations and characters, prompting students to grapple with moral dilemmas and ambiguities. For example, the figure of Shylock is neither a straightforward villain nor a simple victim, encouraging students to question stereotypes, challenge their preconceived notions, and think critically about character portrayal.

Similarly, the play's themes of justice, mercy, prejudice, and friendship provide ample opportunities for critical analysis. Portia's plea for mercy juxtaposed with Shylock's insistence on justice raises questions about the nature of these two values. Is one always superior to the other? Can justice exist without mercy, and vice versa? These questions push students to critically examine their values and assumptions.

The narrative structure, language, and symbolism used in the play also require critical analysis. The parallel plotlines, the use of disguise, the choice of three caskets—all these elements invite students to delve deeper into the text, understand its structure, and appreciate its symbolism. Furthermore, deciphering Shakespeare's language enhances students' comprehension and interpretation skills, bolstering their ability to think critically about text.

While critical thinking enables a cognitive understanding of the text, empathy allows students to connect emotionally with the characters and their experiences. Empathy involves understanding and sharing the feelings of others, a skill that is key to appreciating literature.

Shakespeare's characters in "The Merchant of Venice," despite being from a different era, face emotions and conflicts that are universal: Shylock's anguish at his daughter's desertion, Antonio's melancholy, and Portia's frustration with her lack of agency in choosing her spouse. By empathizing with these characters, students gain insights into human experiences that may differ from their own, fostering tolerance and understanding.

Moreover, empathy plays a significant role in understanding the societal prejudices depicted in the play. While it's important to condemn the anti-Semitic treatment of Shylock, empathizing with his character enables students to fully grasp the devastating impact of prejudice. This empathic understanding can lead to broader discussions about contemporary issues of racism and discrimination.

In conclusion, studying "The Merchant of Venice" fosters both critical thinking and empathy. The play's complex characters and themes encourage students to question, analyze, and form judgments, honing their critical thinking skills. Simultaneously, its exploration of universal human experiences and societal issues offers opportunities for empathic engagement. These cognitive and emotional dimensions complement each other, enriching students' understanding of the text and its relevance to their lives and the world around them.

Engagement with controversial issues

"The Merchant of Venice," one of William Shakespeare's most provocative plays, delves into various controversial issues, including religious intolerance, racial prejudice, patriarchy, materialism, and the tension between justice and mercy. Shakespeare's nuanced engagement with these issues not only reflects the societal norms of his time but also provokes contemporary audiences to question and confront their values and biases.

The issue of religious intolerance is strikingly evident in "The Merchant of Venice." Set in a predominantly Christian Venice, the play portrays the marginalization and mistreatment of Shylock, a Jewish moneylender. This discrimination is institutional and personal, as depicted in Antonio's demeaning treatment of Shylock in Act 1, Scene 3, where he confesses, "I am as like to call thee so again, To spit on thee again, to spurn thee too." This vilification, coupled with Shylock's legal persecution in the courtroom scene, presents a damning picture of religious intolerance. Shakespeare's exploration of this issue encourages audiences to confront religious prejudice, a topic that remains controversial and relevant in contemporary society.

Closely linked with religious intolerance is the issue of racial prejudice. Although the racial identity of Jews as a 'race' in the modern sense was not recognized in the Elizabethan era, the play's depiction of Shylock reflects a racialized form of anti-Semitism. His characterization as greedy and vengeful aligns with harmful Jewish stereotypes, further marginalizing him as the 'Other.' However, Shylock's passionate defense of his humanity in his

"Hath not a Jew eyes?" speech (Act 3, Scene 1) challenges these stereotypes, promoting a reevaluation of racial prejudice.

The patriarchal dynamics in "The Merchant of Venice" bring attention to gender inequality, another controversial issue. Portia and Jessica, the play's main female characters, are subjected to patriarchal control. Portia's marriage is determined by her father's will, and Jessica is trapped in her father Shylock's oppressive household. However, both women challenge their subordinate positions. Portia, in her guise as a male lawyer, commands the courtroom, and Jessica defies her father by eloping with Lorenzo. These subversions critique patriarchal norms and provoke reflection on gender roles and women's agency, a topic that remains contentious in many societies.

"The Merchant of Venice" also grapples with the controversial issue of materialism. The Christian characters, who condemn Shylock for his material greed, are themselves embroiled in the pursuit of wealth. Antonio ventures dangerous sea trades for profit, Bassanio courts Portia primarily for her wealth, and Jessica steals her father's ducats and jewels when she elopes. The play thus exposes the hypocrisy surrounding the denouncement of materialism, prompting audiences to reflect on the moral implications of wealth and material pursuit.

The tension between justice and mercy, central to the play's narrative, engages with the controversial issue of legal ethics. Shylock, seeking revenge for Antonio's abuses, demands strict justice according to his bond's terms. In contrast, Portia, disguised as Balthazar, argues for mercy in her eloquent speech in Act 4, Scene 1, stating, "The quality of mercy is not strained... It blesseth him that gives, and him that takes." The stark contrast between Shylock's legalistic rigidity and Portia's appeal to mercy presents a moral and ethical dilemma that encourages audiences to consider the nature of justice, retribution, and forgiveness.

In conclusion, "The Merchant of Venice" engages with controversial issues such as religious intolerance, racial prejudice, patriarchy, materialism, and legal ethics. Through its complex characters, intricate plot, and resonant themes, the play encourages audiences to confront these issues, challenge their assumptions, and consider their implications. This engagement with controversy attests to the play's enduring relevance and its power to provoke dialogue, reflection, and change.

Mercy versus Justice

"The Merchant of Venice" presents a poignant exploration of the struggle between mercy and justice, both indispensable principles in any society. This exploration reveals a dichotomy that is still keenly relevant in contemporary discourse on jurisprudence and ethics, and in broader societal values and norms.

Justice, as depicted in the play, is associated with the uncompromising Shylock, who persistently clings to the bond he made with Antonio, insisting on receiving the "pound of flesh" he is owed as payment for Antonio's defaulted loan. Shylock's interpretation of justice is grounded in the literal reading of contracts and laws, a notion that is expressed succinctly in his plea to the Duke: "I stand here for law" (Act 4, Scene 1). His justice is retributive and punitive, completely devoid of empathy or compassion. It highlights the principle of 'an eye for an eye', a form of justice that can be unyielding and cruel, yet it adheres to the precise standards of fairness and equivalence.

In contrast, mercy is portrayed as a higher, more divine principle, advocated primarily by Portia, who argues for the value of mercy in her renowned speech: "The quality of mercy is not strained... It blesseth him that gives and him that takes" (Act 4, Scene 1). For Portia, mercy is an act of compassion and forgiveness that goes beyond the strict confines of the law. She speaks of mercy as an attribute of God, making it a virtue of the highest order. Her plea for mercy implies a critique of strict adherence to the law, suggesting that legal justice alone is insufficient to govern human relationships and societies.

Yet, the play presents a distinct irony regarding mercy through Portia's actions. After urging Shylock to show mercy, Portia resorts to a manipulative interpretation of the law to deny him the justice he seeks. She argues that while the bond allows Shylock to take a pound of Antonio's flesh, it does not allow him to shed any blood, nor does it give him any right to more or less than exactly one pound of flesh. If Shylock does any of these things, his entire estate will be forfeited under Venetian law.

This argument, while technically true, is an unexpected and somewhat unnatural interpretation of the bond. Portia's logic shows a deviation from the principle of mercy she has been advocating. Further, in Shylock's subsequent punishment - losing half his property and being forced to convert to Christianity - the law appears far from merciful. Here, Portia's conduct reveals an uneasy tension between her words and actions, calling into question whether the implementation of mercy is as straightforward as her eloquent speech suggests.

Moreover, through the contrasting figures of Shylock and Portia, Shakespeare illustrates how both justice and mercy can be perverted or manipulated. Shylock's form of justice, while aligned with the letter of the law, ignores the spirit of the law and disregards the sanctity of human life. Portia, on the other hand, while advocating mercy, exploits the law to ensure Shylock's ruin. This irony presents a powerful critique of the potential for corruption and bias in the application of justice and mercy.

By creating a stark contrast between mercy and justice, "The Merchant of Venice" encourages audiences to engage in deep reflection on these principles. The play doesn't conclusively favor one over the other, rather it presents the dire consequences of adhering strictly to either one. Too much mercy could potentially lead to anarchy, as it might allow wrongdoings to go unpunished. On the other hand, rigid justice can lack empathy, leading to harsh, sometimes devastating outcomes.

Therefore, "The Merchant of Venice" prompts us to seek a balance between mercy and justice. This balance is something societies and legal systems worldwide grapple with. We must ask ourselves, to what extent should mercy temper justice? Or, to what extent should justice be unyielding in the face of pleas for mercy? The play's exploration of mercy versus justice makes it timeless, for it brings to light questions that remain critical in our ongoing conversations about law, punishment, and societal ethics.

Love and Friendship

"The Merchant of Venice" is as much about love and friendship as it is about justice and mercy. Shakespeare explores these themes in depth, revealing how they intersect with each other and with the socioeconomic structures of the Venetian society. The play presents varied facets of love - romantic, platonic, and material - and highlights how friendship can lead to acts of self-sacrifice, yet also be manipulated for personal gain. In the process, it offers a complex picture of human relationships, inviting the audience to reflect on the true nature of love and friendship.

The friendship between Antonio and Bassanio forms a cornerstone of the narrative. It is a bond characterized by profound loyalty and self-sacrifice. Despite being aware of Bassanio's financial recklessness, Antonio agrees to act as surety for the loan Bassanio seeks to woo Portia. His love for Bassanio is so great that he is willing to risk his life: "My purse, my person, my extremest means / Lie all unlocked to your occasions" (Act 1, Scene 1). In this, Antonio embodies the ideal friend, willing to sacrifice everything for Bassanio's happiness.

Yet, this friendship is not without its complications. Bassanio's repeated borrowing from Antonio suggests an imbalance in their relationship, raising questions about Bassanio's motivations. Does Bassanio value Antonio's friendship purely for its own sake or is it tied to the financial support Antonio provides? This ambiguity adds layers of complexity to their friendship, illustrating how even the closest relationships can be influenced by material considerations.

Romantic love in the play is also multifaceted and often intertwined with material interests. Bassanio's courtship of Portia, for instance, is not driven solely by love. He is as attracted to her wealth as he is to her beauty and intelligence. Bassanio openly admits to Antonio that he hopes marrying Portia will resolve his financial woes: "In Belmont is a lady richly left, / And she is fair" (Act 1, Scene 1). The connection between love and wealth is further highlighted in the casket plot. Portia's suitors must choose between gold, silver, and lead caskets, turning the act of wooing into a material gamble.

Yet, despite this intertwining of love and wealth, the play does not completely diminish the value of romantic love. Portia and Bassanio's relationship, though initiated for material reasons, blossoms into a genuine bond. Bassanio's choice of the lead casket, associated with the risk of losing everything, can be seen as an indication of his true feelings for Portia. Similarly, Jessica's decision to elope with Lorenzo, even at the cost of forsaking her father and her faith, suggests that love can motivate individuals to make significant sacrifices.

However, the play also presents a more cynical view of love, as seen in Jessica and Lorenzo's relationship. Their elopement is facilitated by Jessica's theft of her father's money and jewels. While this enables Jessica to escape her oppressive life, it also places a shadow over their love. Their relationship, like Bassanio's courtship of Portia, is built on a foundation of material wealth. This raises questions about the nature of their love, further complicating the play's depiction of romantic relationships.

Through its varied portrayals of love and friendship, "The Merchant of Venice" offers an intricate exploration of human relationships. It suggests that love and friendship are not purely altruistic or selfless, but are often entangled with issues of wealth and power. Yet, it also affirms the capacity of love and friendship to inspire acts of self-sacrifice and loyalty.

By presenting such a complex picture of love and friendship, the play encourages audiences to reflect on the nature of these relationships in their own lives. It asks us to consider the role of material interests in our relationships and to question the extent to which we are willing to sacrifice for the sake of love or friendship. In this way, "The Merchant of Venice" not only offers a compelling narrative but also prompts a deeper examination of the values and motivations that underpin our personal relationships.

Appearance versus Reality

"The Merchant of Venice" is rich in its exploration of the theme of appearance versus reality, presenting numerous situations where things are not as they seem. Shakespeare uses this theme to challenge the audience's perceptions, revealing the gap between outward appearances and the underlying reality. This theme allows for a deeper understanding of the characters, their motivations, and their moral values, and it is used as a tool to explore more profound themes like hypocrisy, prejudice, and the nature of true justice and mercy.

The plot itself hinges on the disparity between appearance and reality. Bassanio must choose the correct casket to win Portia's hand in marriage. The gold casket bears the inscription, "Who chooseth me shall gain what many men desire" (Act 2, Scene 7), the silver, "Who chooseth me shall get as much as he deserves" (Act 2, Scene 9), and the lead, "Who chooseth me must give and hazard all he hath" (Act 2, Scene 7). Many suitors, deceived by the attractive appearances of the gold and silver caskets, fail to recognize the truth that the modest lead casket conceals. This clever narrative device embodies the theme of appearance versus reality, suggesting that true value often lies beneath an unassuming exterior.

Shakespeare also employs this theme in character development, most notably in the case of Portia and Shylock. Portia appears to be a passive character, her fate determined by her father's will. However, as the play unfolds, she emerges as an intelligent, resourceful woman who manipulates the law to save Antonio, revealing her true strength and agency. Similarly,

Shylock, who initially appears as a stereotypical greedy moneylender, reveals deeper complexities as the play progresses. His famous speech, "Hath not a Jew eyes?" (Act 3, Scene 1), exposes the raw humanity and deep-seated resentment beneath his hardened exterior, challenging the audience's initial perception.

Moreover, the theme of appearance versus reality is vital in illustrating the play's exploration of justice and mercy. On the surface, Venice appears to be a place of fairness and impartiality, yet the treatment of Shylock exposes the deep-rooted prejudice within this seemingly just society. Shylock, seeking justice through the law, is denied his rights and treated with a blatant lack of mercy. Meanwhile, Portia, despite her eloquent speech on mercy, manipulates the law to save Antonio, raising questions about the authenticity of her plea for mercy.

The theme is also central to the play's depiction of love and friendship. Antonio's unquestioning loyalty towards Bassanio appears noble, but it also raises questions about Antonio's judgement, given Bassanio's questionable financial habits. Similarly, Bassanio's courtship of Portia initially seems driven by love, but it soon becomes apparent that financial motives significantly influence his actions.

In its depiction of prejudice, the play again utilizes the theme of appearance versus reality. Characters like Antonio and Gratiano judge Shylock based on his religion and occupation, but Shylock's actions and words reveal that he shares the same emotions and desires as his Christian counterparts. This serves as a critique of societal prejudice and the tendency to judge others based on superficial characteristics.

"The Merchant of Venice", through its exploration of appearance versus reality, exposes the often hidden complexities of society, relationships, and individual characters. It forces the audience to question first impressions and to recognize that reality often differs from outward appearances. This theme contributes to the play's enduring relevance, as it challenges audiences to confront their own prejudices, to question their understanding of justice and mercy, and to recognize the profound complexities of human nature and society.

Prejudice

In "The Merchant of Venice", the theme of prejudice plays a crucial role in shaping the dynamics of characters and their relationships. Shakespeare brilliantly explores prejudice along the lines of religion, race, gender, and social status, underpinning the narrative with powerful commentaries on the destructive nature of these biases and their enduring relevance.

Arguably, the most pronounced form of prejudice is religious discrimination, particularly against Jews. Shylock, the Jewish moneylender, is the primary victim. His character serves to expose the deeply entrenched anti-Semitism in Venetian society. From the outset, Shylock is depicted as an outsider, despised for his religious identity and profession. Antonio, Bassanio, and their friends frequently insult and belittle him, revealing their deep-seated prejudice. Shylock's anger and bitterness are epitomized in his famous monologue: "Hath not a Jew eyes?" (Act 3, Scene 1). Here, Shylock challenges the dehumanizing stereotypes about Jews, asserting their shared humanity with Christians.

This prejudice is institutionalized, forming an integral part of Venetian society and its legal system. When Shylock seeks to exact his bond—his legal right—he is met with hypocrisy and intolerance. The court, supposedly a beacon of justice, becomes a venue for reinforcing societal prejudice. In the end, Shylock is not only denied his bond but also forced to convert to Christianity, a brutal culmination of the religious prejudice against him.

Beyond religious bias, "The Merchant of Venice" also portrays gender prejudice. Despite being intelligent and capable, Portia is subjected to her late father's will, which determines her marital destiny through the casket challenge. This reflects the societal norms of the time, where women's rights and choices were significantly limited. Similarly, Jessica, Shylock's daughter, suffers prejudice in her father's house, leading her to renounce her faith to elope with Lorenzo. These characters underscore the patriarchal prejudices that constrain women's autonomy and agency.

Economic prejudice also permeates the play. Shylock's profession as a moneylender attracts scorn and resentment, revealing Venice's bias against those who operate outside its mainstream economic system. Additionally, Bassanio's pursuit of Portia is motivated as much by her wealth as by love, illustrating societal prejudice towards the poor. Bassanio's desperate need to present himself as a wealthy suitor to win Portia's hand highlights the class prejudices inherent in their society.

The theme of prejudice in "The Merchant of Venice" serves a dual purpose. Firstly, it offers a critique of the biases prevalent in Elizabethan society. Through Shylock, Portia, and Bassanio, Shakespeare critiques religious, gender, and economic prejudices, highlighting their destructive consequences. Secondly, the theme encourages audiences to reflect on their prejudices. The contrasting portrayal of characters like Shylock and Antonio compels audiences to challenge their perceptions and to acknowledge the unfairness of prejudice.

Shakespeare also underscores the cyclical nature of prejudice. Shylock's insistence on claiming his pound of flesh can be seen as a response to the years of discrimination he has faced. However, his action only reinforces the Christian community's negative stereotypes of Jews, thereby perpetuating the cycle of prejudice and animosity. This serves as a cautionary tale about the self-perpetuating nature of bias and its potential to breed conflict and injustice.

"The Merchant of Venice", through its exploration of prejudice, illuminates the complexities of societal biases and their implications for justice, mercy, and human relationships. It prompts us to question our prejudices and to recognize the essential humanity shared by all, regardless of religion, gender, or economic status. It forces us to confront the uncomfortable truth that prejudice often lies at the heart of societal conflicts and injustices, a message as relevant today as it was in Shakespeare's time.

—·—

INTERPLAY OF RELIGIOUS AND SECULAR LAW

In "The Merchant of Venice," the interplay of religious and secular law is a prominent theme, driving both the narrative and the characterization of the key players. Shakespeare masterfully juxtaposes these two legal frameworks, each represented by Christian and Jewish characters, to examine their underlying principles, contradictions, and the conflicts they generate. The play thus invites the audience to reflect on the nature of justice, mercy, and the moral and ethical dilemmas that arise when religious and secular laws collide.

Secular law is represented by Venice's civil law, which prides itself on its impartiality and adherence to contract law. It's this system that allows Shylock to demand a pound of Antonio's flesh as repayment for his defaulted loan, despite the horrifying implications. Antonio has willingly entered into this contract, and therefore, as per Venetian law, he is obliged to honor it.

On the other hand, the Christian characters, particularly Portia, represent the religious law—Christianity's ethical teachings of love, mercy, and forgiveness. These principles clash starkly with the harsh legalism of the bond. Yet, it's important to note that these Christian characters are not entirely consistent in their adherence to these teachings. They're quick to condemn Shylock for his lack of mercy, but they themselves show no mercy toward him, both in their personal interactions and in the court.

The trial scene (Act 4, Scene 1) is the crux of this interplay between religious and secular law. Portia, disguised as a lawyer, initially seems to uphold the Venetian law, stating, "Then must the Jew be merciful...On what compulsion must I? Tell me that" (Act 4, Scene 1), thereby implying that mercy cannot be legally enforced but is a moral choice. However, she turns the secular law on its head with a technicality, stating that the bond allows Shylock to cut a pound of flesh but not to shed any Christian blood. If he does so, his life and goods are forfeit under Venetian law. Here, secular law, with a religious twist, is used to ensure Antonio's survival and Shylock's defeat.

This manipulation of secular law also brings to the fore the bias within the ostensibly neutral legal system. Shylock, despite his legal rights, is denied justice due to his religious identity, exposing the deep-seated Christian bias in the Venetian law. Furthermore, Shylock is forced to convert to Christianity, which presents a violation of religious freedom, adding to the critique of the hypocrisy and prejudice embedded in the law.

Interestingly, Shakespeare uses this interplay of religious and secular law to reveal character. Antonio, a devout Christian, willingly submits to the secular law, ready to sacrifice his life to honor his bond. On the other hand, Shylock, driven by the desire for revenge and legalism, rigidly sticks to the letter of the contract until the end. Portia, while initially appearing to uphold the secular law, skillfully manipulates it to align with the religious principle of mercy (or at least a form of it), revealing her intelligence and resourcefulness.

Through this exploration of religious and secular law, "The Merchant of Venice" provokes thought on the complexity of justice. It underscores the importance of mercy in justice, challenging a strictly legalistic approach. However, it also highlights the potential for bias and prejudice in the application of both religious and secular law, warning of the injustices that can arise when these laws are applied without genuine understanding and empathy.

Ultimately, the play does not offer a straightforward resolution to the conflict between religious and secular law. Instead, it leaves the audience with a nuanced understanding of the complexities and potential pitfalls in the pursuit of justice. It challenges us to consider how we might navigate these complexities in our societies, promoting dialogue and reflection on the balance between law, morality, and mercy.

MATERIAL WEALTH VS HUMAN VALUE

"The Merchant of Venice" is marked by a profound exploration of the theme of material wealth versus human value. Throughout the play, Shakespeare juxtaposes the pursuit of wealth with the intrinsic worth of human beings, relationships, and moral virtues. This theme provokes reflection on the value we assign to material possessions and the ways in which they influence our relationships, self-perception, and judgement of others.

The primary plotline of the play - Antonio's bond with Shylock - provides a clear manifestation of this theme. Antonio, a well-respected merchant, is ready to stake his life on a pound of flesh to secure a loan for his friend Bassanio, reflecting the fact that he values friendship more than his own life. On the other hand, Shylock, a Jewish moneylender, uses the loan to assert his value, using the bond as a means of revenge against Antonio's insults and the wider prejudice he faces as a Jew in Venice.

In Bassanio's quest for Portia's hand in marriage, the theme of wealth versus human value is again at the forefront. Bassanio is initially drawn to Portia for her wealth, viewing it as a solution to his financial woes. This superficial pursuit of wealth leads him to risk his friend's life, raising questions about his values and the human cost of his ambitions. However, his successful choice of the lead casket indicates a realization of the worth of inner virtues over outward wealth - "The world is still deceived with ornament" (Act 3, Scene 2).

Portia herself, a wealthy heiress, struggles with the challenge of material wealth versus human value. Despite her riches, she is bound by her father's will and unable to choose her husband, suggesting that wealth can be a cage rather than a liberator. This predicament forces her to evaluate her suitors based on their character rather than their wealth, aligning her with the theme of human value.

Shakespeare also explores this theme through Jessica, Shylock's daughter. She forsakes her father, her faith, and her heritage - symbolized by her theft of Shylock's ducats and the turquoise ring - to elope with Lorenzo. While her actions can be interpreted as a rejection of material wealth in favor of love, they also come with a significant human cost - her relationship with her father and her cultural identity.

"The Merchant of Venice" prompts us to question how we measure value - in terms of gold or in terms of goodness. The Christian characters, despite their claims of moral superiority, often allow material wealth to dictate their actions. Antonio risks his life for Bassanio's debt, Bassanio courts Portia for her fortune, and Jessica steals from her father to elope with Lorenzo. Conversely, Shylock, despite his occupation as a moneylender, seeks to assert his human value in a society that reduces him to his profession and faith.

Yet, the resolution of the play presents a somewhat complex message. On the one hand, Shylock, who seeks to trade a pound of flesh (human value) for his ducats (material wealth), is defeated, while Portia and Bassanio, who learn to value human relationships over wealth, achieve a happy ending. However, Antonio, whose life was gambled for the sake of wealth, is saved but remains indebted, and Shylock is stripped of his wealth and forced to convert, suggesting a grim outcome for those who cannot navigate the tension between wealth and human value.

In conclusion, "The Merchant of Venice" uses the theme of material wealth versus human value to critique societal values and provoke thought on what we value and why. It reminds us of the dangers of allowing wealth to cloud our judgement, the importance of recognizing the intrinsic worth of individuals beyond their economic status, and the need for a balance between material pursuits and moral and human values. This theme, explored with Shakespeare's characteristic depth and nuance, contributes to the enduring relevance of the play.

Summary of the Play

"The Merchant of Venice" is one of William Shakespeare's most renowned plays, a work rich in compelling characters and intricate themes. As we dive into the world of this play, we encounter a world of love, friendship, justice, mercy, and the often blurred lines between appearance and reality.

The play opens in Venice, Italy, where the melancholic Antonio, a wealthy merchant, is discussing his sadness with his friends. The source of his melancholy is never clearly identified, but it is inferred it could be due to his friend Bassanio's courting of a wealthy heiress named Portia, which he supports but seems to leave him in emotional distress. Bassanio, who is financially strapped, requires three thousand ducats to support his quest for Portia's hand. He asks Antonio for help. Antonio, having tied up his money in shipping ventures, suggests borrowing the money from moneylenders using his ships as collateral.

Bassanio approaches the Jewish moneylender, Shylock, who proposes an unusual bond. Given Antonio's repeated insults and prejudice against him, Shylock proposes that if the loan is not repaid by the agreed date, he will be entitled to a pound of Antonio's flesh. Assured of the return of his ships long before the due date, Antonio agrees to this contract, so that Bassanio can court Portia with the necessary finances.

Meanwhile, in Belmont, Portia is dealing with her own predicament. She is bound by her late father's will to marry the man who correctly chooses among three caskets - one gold, one silver, and one lead. Numerous suitors from various countries attempt and fail this trial. When Bassanio arrives, aided by the money from Antonio's bond, he chooses correctly, picking the lead casket, and wins Portia's hand in marriage. During this time, Bassanio's friend Gratiano also falls in love with and becomes engaged to Portia's maid, Nerissa.

Trouble arises when news reaches Belmont that Antonio's ships have been wrecked and he cannot repay the bond. Shylock, who is bitter about his daughter Jessica eloping with a Christian named Lorenzo and taking a portion of his wealth, insists on exacting his bond, ignoring pleas for mercy.

In the dramatic courtroom scene, the Duke presiding over the case is sympathetic to Antonio but states that he cannot annul a contract. As all hope seems lost, a young law clerk, Balthazar (Portia in disguise), arrives, supposedly sent by the learned lawyer Bellario, at the Duke's request. Balthazar argues for mercy, but when Shylock refuses, she initially seems to support Shylock's claim, stating that the bond is legally binding.

Just as Shylock is about to cut Antonio's flesh, Balthazar points out that the bond doesn't grant him any drop of blood – only flesh. If Shylock were to shed any blood in the process of obtaining his pound of flesh, he would be guilty of conspiring against the life of a Venetian citizen and his life and goods would be at the mercy of the Duke and Antonio. Shylock finds himself caught in his own trap and is asked to show the mercy he himself had denied. When he tries to take the money instead, he is denied this as well, having already refused it in court. As punishment, he is forced to sign over his property to Jessica and Lorenzo and convert to Christianity.

With Shylock's defeat, Antonio is saved, and the lovers - Portia and Bassanio, Nerissa and Gratiano, and Jessica and Lorenzo - rejoice. However, the play ends on a somewhat melancholic note as Antonio remains a lonely figure, a contrast to the pairs of lovers, suggesting that the play's conflicts and tensions are not fully resolved.

In the play, Shakespeare deftly intertwines narratives of love, justice, friendship, and prejudice, making "The Merchant of Venice" a multi-layered exploration of human nature and society. It raises pertinent questions about the justice system, religious tensions, the power of love and sacrifice, and societal attitudes towards wealth and status. The richness of its character development, narrative structure, thematic depth, and its blend of tragedy and comedy make it one of Shakespeare's most intriguing plays.

— · —

ACT I

"The Merchant of Venice" Act 1 is composed of three scenes. Here's a detailed scene-by-scene summary:

Scene 1

The play opens on a street in Venice, where the merchant Antonio is in conversation with his friends Salarino and Solanio. Antonio expresses a profound sadness he doesn't understand. His friends propose that his melancholy might be due to his worries about his merchant ships at sea, carrying his investment, or perhaps because he is in love. Antonio dismisses both hypotheses but fails to articulate why he's feeling the way he does.

As they are talking, Bassanio, Lorenzo, and Gratiano join them. Once Salarino and Solanio exit, Bassanio shares his plan with Antonio to court a wealthy heiress named Portia who lives in Belmont. Bassanio confesses that he has squandered his wealth and seeks Antonio's financial support in his quest for Portia. Antonio, without cash himself because his wealth is tied up in his shipping ventures, promises to help Bassanio secure a loan using Antonio's credit.

Scene 2

The scene shifts to Belmont, in the house of Portia. Portia is talking to her waiting woman, Nerissa, about the discomfort she feels regarding the terms of her father's will. Her father's will dictates that her future husband should be the one who chooses the correct casket among three (made of gold, silver, and lead) - each containing clues leading to the correct choice. She speaks of her numerous suitors, none of whom she particularly likes.

She would prefer to choose her husband herself rather than rely on the casket lottery.

Nerissa recalls a Venetian man, Bassanio, who visited before Portia's father died. Portia remembers him fondly, hinting at her interest in him. A servant interrupts them with the news that five more suitors have arrived. Though Portia is not excited about the prospect, she decides to greet them with Nerissa.

Scene 3

Back in Venice, Bassanio and Shylock, a Jewish moneylender, are in discussion about the loan of three thousand ducats Bassanio seeks. Shylock expresses his reservations about Antonio's guarantee since all Antonio's assets are at sea. He also reflects on the many times Antonio has berated him for his usury, a typical business for Jews in a time when Christian law forbade them from most other occupations.

Despite his past encounters with Antonio, Shylock proposes the terms of the loan: if the loan is not repaid within three months, Shylock is entitled to a pound of Antonio's flesh. Bassanio is shocked at these terms but Shylock insists it's in a "merry sport" and thus, they agree. Antonio arrives and the men proceed to finalize the bond, leading to one of the most dramatic plotlines in the play.

The first act sets the stage for the tensions and dilemmas that unfurl later in the play, introducing key themes and character relationships. It foreshadows the dangerous bond that Antonio is willing to enter into for the sake of his friend, and the lengths Bassanio will go to secure his love interest, Portia. Meanwhile, Portia's plight of being unable to choose her husband freely introduces a plotline that explores themes of destiny, choice, and appearance versus reality.

ACT 2

"The Merchant of Venice" Act 2 contains nine scenes, which further develop the plot and deepen the stakes for the characters. Here's a detailed scene-by-scene summary:

Scene 1

In Belmont, the Moroccan prince chooses the gold casket, believing that it will win him Portia. The gold casket's inscription reads, "Who chooseth me shall gain what many men desire," but instead of finding a picture of Portia inside, he finds a skull. Portia shows him out politely, relieved that he chose wrong.

Scene 2

Back in Venice, Launcelot Gobbo, a comical character and servant to Shylock, debates whether to stay with his master. His conscience tells him to stay, but his sense of ambition urges him to leave. He encounters his blind father, Old Gobbo, and decides to play a cruel trick by claiming that Launcelot is dead. But soon, he reveals his identity and informs his father about his intention to leave Shylock's service.

Bassanio enters and Launcelot requests to work for him instead. Bassanio agrees, and Launcelot runs off to invite Shylock to dinner, leaving Bassanio to chat with Old Gobbo, who gives Bassanio a basket of doves as a present.

Scene 3

In Shylock's house, Jessica, Shylock's daughter, bids farewell to Launcelot, sad to see him leave. She gives him a letter to deliver to Lorenzo, a Christian friend of Bassanio, with whom she's in love. She expresses her sadness over being the daughter of Shylock and her plans to convert to Christianity and elope with Lorenzo.

Scene 4

At a street in Venice, Gratiano, Lorenzo, Salarino, and Solanio make plans to attend Bassanio's feast. Lorenzo receives Jessica's letter from Launcelot, outlining her plans to escape her father's house and elope with Lorenzo.

Scene 5

Back at Shylock's house, Launcelot and Jessica joke around before Shylock, suspicious and grumpy, intervenes. He criticizes Launcelot's new service to Bassanio, warns Jessica to guard their house and not to be a gazing stock for the Christian revelers, and leaves for dinner with Bassanio.

Scene 6

In Venice, Gratiano and Salarino wait for Lorenzo near Shylock's house. Jessica arrives disguised as a boy, carrying a chest full of her father's ducats and jewels. When Lorenzo arrives, they exchange expressions of love and leave, with Jessica feeling guilty about her actions.

Scene 7

Back in Belmont, the Prince of Arragon is presented with the casket test. He dismisses the gold casket, thinking he's better than what many men desire, and the lead one as he wouldn't risk all he has for what could be nothing. He picks the silver casket, but instead of Portia's picture, it contains a fool's head, indicating he made the wrong choice. The Prince leaves Belmont.

Scene 8

Back in Venice, Salarino and Solanio discuss the elopement of Jessica and Lorenzo, express their worry about Antonio's ventures, and plan to meet with Bassanio and Gratiano, who are about to set sail for Belmont.

Scene 9

In Belmont, a servant informs Portia that a young Venetian, presumably Bassanio, has arrived. While Portia hopes it's Bassanio, she maintains her outward composure. Meanwhile, Nerissa and the servant discuss the drunkenness of Gratiano, who has accompanied the Venetian.

The second act further develops the character relationships and adds more tension and drama, from the continuing suitors' failure to choose the right casket to Jessica's controversial elopement. The various settings of Belmont and Venice serve to contrast the world of wealth, love, and chance with the world of commerce, law, and prejudice.

ACT 3

"The Merchant of Venice" Act 3 consists of five scenes, and it's where the plot significantly advances, and the stakes become higher. Here's a detailed scene-by-scene summary:

Scene 1

In Venice, Salanio and Salarino discuss the loss of Antonio's ship. Shylock enters, lamenting the loss of his daughter and his ducats, equating both losses. He blames the Christians for aiding Jessica's escape and expresses his desire for revenge against Antonio, both for his own humiliation and for Antonio's mistreatment of him. When Tubal, a friend of Shylock, brings news of Jessica spending Shylock's money and the potential ruin of Antonio, Shylock gleefully plans to exact his bond.

Scene 2

In Belmont, Bassanio prepares to choose the casket. Portia urges him to delay his choice, fearful he might choose incorrectly. But Bassanio proceeds, dismissing the gold and silver caskets and choosing lead, expressing that outward appearances can often hide the true value within. He finds Portia's portrait inside, and they exchange vows of love. A joyful Portia gives him a ring as a token of their love, making him promise never to lose it or give it away.

Gratiano, who has accompanied Bassanio, announces his intention to marry Nerissa. Their happiness is interrupted by Lorenzo's letter informing them of Antonio's losses and Shylock's intention to exact his bond. Despite Portia's wish for Bassanio to stay longer, she understands his obligation to help Antonio, so she gives him money to repay the loan and plans to live in a monastery while Bassanio is away.

Scene 3

Back in Venice, Shylock escorts Antonio to jail, insisting on the repayment of the bond despite Bassanio's offer to repay it tenfold. Shylock is adamant about taking his revenge and refuses to listen to Antonio's pleas. Antonio resignedly accepts his fate, saying he's prepared for death.

Scene 4

In Belmont, after Bassanio and Gratiano leave for Venice, Lorenzo reassures Portia about Antonio's fate. After Lorenzo and Jessica exit to walk in the garden, Portia reveals her plan to Nerissa. They decide to go to Venice disguised as men to help save Antonio. Portia instructs her servant to inform any visitors that they have gone to a monastery.

Scene 5

In Belmont, Launcelot teases Jessica about her Jewish origins, and Lorenzo defends her. They engage in a playful discourse on sin, damnation, and salvation before going inside for dinner at Portia's request.

In this act, the full extent of Shylock's wrath and thirst for revenge is revealed, while the lovers Bassanio and Portia are finally united in marriage. However, the looming threat over Antonio's life casts a shadow over their happiness. Meanwhile, Portia's decision to disguise herself as a male lawyer and intervene in Antonio's case introduces a dramatic turn of events, adding to the suspense and anticipation of the climax.

ACT 4

Act 4 of "The Merchant of Venice" contains two scenes, with the first being one of the most dramatic in the entire play. Here's a detailed scene-by-scene summary:

Scene 1

The Duke of Venice presides over Antonio's trial, urging Shylock to show mercy but to no avail. Bassanio and Gratiano, newly married and unaware of their wives' disguise plan, arrive and offer to pay Shylock the owed sum and more. However, Shylock insists on exacting his bond – a pound of Antonio's flesh.

A young lawyer (Portia in disguise) and his clerk (Nerissa in disguise) arrive, armed with a letter of recommendation from the respected lawyer Bellario. Portia (as the lawyer Balthazar) gives a moving speech about the quality of mercy, again urging Shylock to pardon the debt. When Shylock refuses, she initially seems to uphold Shylock's claim, stating the law allows him to claim a pound of Antonio's flesh.

Just when Shylock is about to carve the flesh from Antonio, Portia points out that the bond doesn't allow Shylock to spill any Christian blood. Since it's impossible to cut a pound of flesh without shedding blood, Shylock's attempt to claim his bond would lead to his own death as per Venetian law. Defeated, Shylock agrees to take Bassanio's offer of money, but Portia insists that Shylock should get only the penalty stipulated in the bond. In the end, due to Venetian laws against threatening a citizen's life, Shylock loses half his property to Antonio and the state.

Antonio relinquishes his share on two conditions: Shylock must convert to Christianity and leave his remaining property to Jessica and Lorenzo after his death. Shylock exits, broken and ruined.

Subsequently, Bassanio and Gratiano thank the young lawyer and his clerk, offering rich rewards. As tokens of their gratitude, Portia and Nerissa ask for and receive the rings they gave their husbands earlier, thereby setting the stage for a playful subplot.

Scene 2

In Belmont, Lorenzo and Jessica share a romantic moment under the moonlight. A messenger arrives and announces the imminent return of Portia and Nerissa, causing Lorenzo to order music and preparations to welcome them. Portia and Nerissa arrive, and while Portia comments on the sweet sound of the music, they prepare to reveal their adventure and confront their husbands about the missing rings.

In this act, Shylock's plot for revenge backfires spectacularly due to Portia's intellectual maneuvering. The act explores themes of mercy, justice, and the power of interpretation, while injecting elements of comic relief through the ring subplot. The climactic courtroom scene not only resolves the conflict between Antonio and Shylock but also sets the stage for the final act of the play.

— · —

ACT 5

Act 5 of "The Merchant of Venice" consists of a single scene, but it's rich with resolution, reconciliation, and humor. Here's a detailed summary:

Scene 1

In Belmont, outside Portia's house, Lorenzo and Jessica enjoy a romantic moment, discussing famous lovers from classical stories. They also share a peaceful moment stargazing and enjoying the tranquillity of the night.

As Launcelot delivers the news that Bassanio and his party are returning, Portia and Nerissa approach, engaging in a playful discourse on their husbands' loyalty. Bassanio, Antonio, and Gratiano enter, and Portia welcomes them warmly. The women then start to playfully chide their husbands about the rings they'd given away.

Gratiano quickly admits that he gave his ring to the clerk (Nerissa in disguise), reasoning it was a small price to pay for Antonio's life. Nerissa, feigning anger, claims that the clerk was actually herself, and she spent the night with Gratiano.

Bassanio is then put on the spot about his ring. He admits to giving it to the young lawyer (Portia in disguise), causing Portia to playfully tease him, stating the lawyer's clerk had slept with her. As the men stand in stunned silence, Portia reveals that she was, in fact, the lawyer and Nerissa was the clerk, and they were testing their husbands' loyalty.

Subsequently, Antonio's lost ships are reported to have safely arrived in Venice, providing a final happy ending. The couples reconcile, and they all go into the house to discuss their adventures in detail, ending the play on a note of harmony and resolution.

In this final act, the ring subplot reaches its humorous conclusion. The act provides a balance to the intense courtroom drama of Act 4 with its romantic atmosphere and comic misunderstandings. As the characters reunite, share their adventures, and resolve their conflicts, Shakespeare gives us a delightful and satisfying resolution to the complexities of the plot.

— • —

PLOT

"The Merchant of Venice," is a tale of love, friendship, money, and justice set against the backdrop of the vibrant city-state of Venice and the romantic Belmont.

The play begins with Antonio, a wealthy Venetian merchant, feeling inexplicably sad. His friends suggest his mind is probably on his ships carrying goods that are still at sea. However, Antonio denies it. The conversation switches when Bassanio, Antonio's friend, confesses he needs a loan to court the wealthy heiress Portia, but Antonio's funds are tied up in his fleet. Regardless, he supports Bassanio's pursuit and suggests they secure a loan using his ships as collateral.

In Belmont, Portia is frustrated by her deceased father's will, which states she must marry the man who chooses the correct one of three caskets – gold, silver, or lead. Suitors from around the world visit, but none have been successful, and Portia remains unwed.

Bassanio and Antonio approach Shylock, a Jewish moneylender, for the loan. Shylock, having been publicly insulted and despised by Antonio due to his usury and Jewish faith, proposes a deal. He will lend the money interest-free, but if it's not repaid by the due date, Shylock will take a pound of Antonio's flesh.

Bassanio travels to Belmont and chooses the correct casket, the lead one, thereby winning Portia's hand in marriage. In a parallel romantic subplot, Portia's maid, Nerissa, gets engaged to Bassanio's friend, Gratiano.

Back in Venice, things turn sour when Antonio's ships are reported lost at sea, leaving him unable to repay the loan. A thrilled Shylock demands his bond be fulfilled as revenge for Antonio's previous mistreatment. Antonio is arrested and brought to court.

Meanwhile, Jessica, Shylock's daughter, elopes with Lorenzo, a friend of Antonio and Bassanio, converting to Christianity and taking a significant amount of Shylock's fortune, further fueling Shylock's anger.

Hearing about Antonio's plight, Portia disguises herself as a male lawyer and arrives in Venice's court with Nerissa, disguised as her clerk. After failing to persuade Shylock to show mercy, Portia cleverly points out that Shylock's bond only allows him to take Antonio's flesh, not his blood. Since it's impossible to take flesh without spilling blood, Shylock's claim is denied. Shylock is then punished for his attempt on Antonio's life.

Back in Belmont, Portia and Nerissa tease their husbands about giving away their wedding rings to the disguised women. All misunderstandings are resolved when Portia and Nerissa reveal their disguise. The play concludes with news that Antonio's ships have arrived safely after all, and the couples retire to bed, ending on a happy note.

The play intertwines themes of friendship, love, and the harsh justice of the law, prejudice, and mercy in a tightly woven plot, making it one of Shakespeare's most compelling plays.

—·—

MAIN CHARACTERS

"The Merchant of Venice" features several important characters, each of whom plays a significant role in the development of the story. The main characters include:

1. **Antonio**: Antonio is a wealthy Venetian merchant whose generosity and kindness towards his friend Bassanio set the main plot in motion. Despite his apparent goodness, Antonio is shown to harbor deep prejudice against Shylock, the Jewish moneylender.

2. **Bassanio**: Bassanio is Antonio's friend who borrows money from him to woo Portia, the heiress of Belmont. Despite his financial difficulties, he is portrayed as a noble and loyal friend.

3. **Portia**: Portia is a wealthy heiress from Belmont. She is bound by her father's will to marry the man who correctly chooses one of three caskets. Portia is known for her intelligence, wit, and beauty, all of which are displayed when she disguises herself as a male lawyer to save Antonio.

4. **Shylock**: Shylock is a Jewish moneylender in Venice. He is often mistreated because of his religion and profession. When Antonio fails to repay a loan, Shylock insists on exacting a pound of Antonio's flesh as per their agreement, revealing his desire for revenge against Antonio's insults and abuses.

5. **Jessica**: Jessica is Shylock's daughter who elopes with Lorenzo, taking a significant amount of her father's wealth. She is unhappy with her life in her father's home and converts to Christianity after eloping.

6. **Lorenzo**: Lorenzo is a friend of Antonio and Bassanio and is in love with Jessica. He helps Jessica escape her father's house and they elope together.

7. **Gratiano**: Gratiano is another friend of Antonio and Bassanio who accompanies Bassanio to Belmont. He is known for his talkative and jovial nature and falls in love with Nerissa, Portia's maid.

8. **Nerissa**: Nerissa is Portia's lady-in-waiting. Like her mistress, she also disguises herself, as a law clerk, during the trial in Venice. She marries Gratiano.

These main characters, through their interwoven relationships and conflicts, bring to life the themes of love, justice, mercy, prejudice, and friendship that are central to the play.

Describe Antonio

Antonio, the eponymous Merchant of Venice in William Shakespeare's play, is a complex character whose motivations, emotions, and actions serve as the driving force behind the narrative. The contours of his character are primarily shaped by the interplay of his roles as a merchant, friend, and adversary, and the different relationships he shares with other characters.

Antonio, as his title suggests, is a merchant in the bustling city-state of Venice. His trade forms an essential part of his identity and his wealth affords him influence and respect. Yet, he is presented as a man of melancholy at the beginning of the play, "In sooth, I know not why I am so sad" (Act 1, Scene 1). His profession requires him to send his ships far and wide, rendering his wealth and wellbeing subject to the unpredictable elements, exemplifying the precarious nature of merchant life in the Elizabethan era.

However, Antonio's character is not defined solely by his professional life; he is also shown to be a generous and loyal friend. His relationship with Bassanio, marked by selfless devotion, is integral to the plot. Bassanio's need for money to woo Portia triggers Antonio's decision to borrow from Shylock, and he even stakes a pound of his flesh as guarantee. Antonio's readiness to risk his life for a friend is an act of exceptional loyalty, showing him as a person who values friendship above all.

On the other hand, Antonio's relationship with Shylock, the Jewish moneylender, brings out a different side of his character – a man capable of prejudice and cruelty. He admits to have scorned Shylock for his usury and ethnicity, "I am as like to call thee so again, to spit on thee again, to spurn thee too" (Act 1, Scene 3). His prejudice against Shylock adds layers to his character, revealing a man trapped in the religious biases of his time.

Antonio's character evolves significantly throughout the play, especially in the courtroom scene, where he faces the prospect of death with dignity and courage. He bids Bassanio farewell, prepared to die for his friend: "Commend me to your honourable wife: tell her the process of Antonio's end" (Act 4, Scene 1). Antonio's calm acceptance of his fate portrays him as a tragic figure with stoic resolve.

Yet, his sense of justice prevails when he demands, as Shylock's punishment, that Shylock convert to Christianity and leave his wealth to Jessica and Lorenzo. Here, Antonio reveals his ability to be both merciful and harsh – sparing Shylock's life, but at the cost of Shylock's faith and property.

As a character, Antonio embodies several contradictions. He is a successful merchant burdened with melancholy, a loyal friend and a cruel adversary. His generosity and deep sense of friendship are juxtaposed against his religious intolerance, offering a multi-faceted character whose actions and relationships drive the plot of the play. He displays magnanimity and prejudice, courage and vulnerability, evoking a range of responses from the audience.

Furthermore, Antonio's character serves as a mirror to the societal norms and values of the Elizabethan era, reflecting the era's mercantile pursuits, its notions of friendship and honor, and its religious bigotry. His interactions with characters like Bassanio and Shylock expose societal dynamics of the time, from the platonic male friendships to the deep-rooted anti-Semitism.

Antonio's character ultimately is a testament to Shakespeare's ability to create complex characters who are both a product of their time and yet resonate with audiences across centuries. His complex persona, defined by loyalty, prejudice, courage, and vulnerability, provides audiences with rich material for exploration and analysis. Antonio, the melancholic merchant, the selfless friend, the prejudiced adversary, and the dignified man facing death, remains a compelling figure in the world of Shakespearean drama.

Though his fate improves at the end of the play when his lost ships are reported safe, Antonio's story leaves a lasting impression. His character offers profound insights into human nature, friendship, bias, and justice, making him one of the most memorable characters in Shakespeare's oeuvre. By embodying a spectrum of virtues and vices, Antonio serves as a potent symbol of the human condition, making "The Merchant of Venice" a timeless exploration of humanity.

DESCRIBE BASSANIO

Bassanio, one of the key characters in William Shakespeare's "The Merchant of Venice," presents an intriguing blend of qualities that range from romantic aspiration and filial loyalty to practical wisdom and noble friendship. As the suitor to Portia and Antonio's close friend, Bassanio is instrumental in setting the play's plot in motion and navigating its central themes.

When Bassanio is introduced, he's a young Venetian of noble rank but with a penchant for living beyond his means. He embodies the youthful, adventurous spirit of the age, a man passionate and prone to excesses: "Till I have brought thee where thou wouldst go, to have it every debt that I do owe" (Act 1, Scene 1). Despite these faults, he retains a certain charm and sense of honor, traits that endear him to Antonio and eventually to Portia.

His pursuit of Portia is initially perceived as mercenary due to his dire financial state. Yet, as the play unfolds, Bassanio's genuine love for Portia is revealed, dismissing the notion of his motivations being solely pecuniary. His speech during the casket challenge, where he chooses lead over gold and silver, demonstrates his understanding of the deceptive nature of appearances: "The world is still deceived with ornament" (Act 3, Scene 2). This reveals his wisdom and depth, and his ability to see beyond the superficial.

Bassanio's friendship with Antonio forms a central pillar of his character. It is his financial request that prompts Antonio to borrow money from Shylock, thus triggering the play's major conflict. His deep affection and gratitude towards Antonio are evident in the way he rushes back to Venice upon hearing about Antonio's predicament, ready to give up everything, even his newly married wife, for his friend's safety: "Myself, my wife and all the world, are not with me esteemed above thy life" (Act 4, Scene 1). This powerful portrayal of friendship showcases Bassanio's loyalty and the depth of his character.

Bassanio's relationship with Shylock is limited but pivotal. It is for his sake that Antonio enters the hazardous bond, thereby turning Shylock into their mutual adversary. Despite his limited direct interaction with Shylock, Bassanio serves as a counterpoint to Shylock's pursuit of material and legal justice, underscoring the play's exploration of mercy, friendship, and the human spirit.

Bassanio's character also raises the theme of fortune versus merit. His successful wooing of Portia and the luck that aids him in his choice of the correct casket highlight the role of fortune in human endeavors. Despite his debts, Bassanio's good qualities ultimately help him achieve his goal, suggesting that while fortune plays a role, it is character and wisdom that eventually count.

While Bassanio isn't a flawless hero, his combination of attributes—nobility, love, wisdom, loyalty, and a dash of fortune—make him an engaging and essential character. His romantic relationship with Portia, deep friendship with Antonio, and the resulting conflict with Shylock create a dynamic narrative matrix that embodies the drama's core themes.

As a character, Bassanio encapsulates the struggles, values, and aspirations of a young nobleman in the bustling milieu of Renaissance Venice. His journey from a debt-ridden suitor to a devoted husband and savior-friend explores the human capacity for growth and redemption.

In conclusion, Bassanio is a richly drawn character whose charm, wisdom, loyalty, and capacity for love bring a nuanced depth to "The Merchant of Venice". His role offers insights into the era's societal dynamics, its perspectives on friendship, love, and wealth, and its grappling with the human condition. Through Bassanio, Shakespeare explores the entwined destinies of love and friendship, merit and fortune, presenting a timeless character whose struggles and triumphs continue to resonate with audiences.

Describe Portia

Portia, the radiant heroine of Shakespeare's "The Merchant of Venice," is a paragon of beauty, intelligence, and virtue. Her character embodies a myriad of roles – a dutiful daughter, a discerning lover, a deft lawyer, and a loyal friend, each contributing significantly to the richness of the plot and the play's enduring appeal.

Portia first appears as a wealthy heiress from Belmont, bound by her late father's will to marry the man who correctly chooses one of three caskets – gold, silver, and lead. This device, while limiting her autonomy, also serves to showcase her obedience and respect for her father's wisdom: "I may neither choose who I would nor refuse who I dislike; so is the will of a living daughter curbed by the will of a dead father" (Act 1, Scene 2). Her submission to her father's will demonstrates her dutifulness and respect for the societal norms of her time.

While bound by her father's will, Portia is not without discernment or agency in matters of love. Her conversation with Nerissa reveals her assessment of her suitors, showing her to be perceptive and intelligent. Her joy at Bassanio's arrival and her subtle hint to choose the right casket suggest that her heart has its own preference. Her relief and happiness when Bassanio chooses the lead casket affirm her love for him: "You see me, Lord Bassanio, where I stand, such as I am" (Act 3, Scene 2). Here, Portia emerges not just as a passive recipient of fortune, but as an active participant in her destiny.

Portia's most celebrated role, perhaps, is her appearance in the court of Venice, disguised as a young lawyer. Her ingenious interpretation of the law, her eloquence, and her triumphant plea for mercy – "The quality of mercy is not strained" (Act 4, Scene 1) – underscore her intellectual prowess and moral rectitude. By saving Antonio's life, she establishes herself as a beacon of justice and mercy, marking one of the most iconic moments in the play.

Even as she exercises justice, Portia's conduct is marked by a playful sense of humor, most evident in the final act, where she teases Bassanio about the missing ring. She manipulates the situation expertly, creating a humorous tension before revealing her secret: "I was the doctor, Nerissa there his clerk" (Act 5, Scene 1). This scene showcases her wit, further enhancing the complexity of her character.

Portia's role also reflects the gender dynamics and societal expectations of the Elizabethan era. Even though she is subject to the whims of a patriarchal society, she manages to assert herself within its confines. Her subversion of gender norms, especially when she assumes the role of a male lawyer, provides a counterpoint to the traditional female roles of her time. This emphasizes Shakespeare's ability to create strong female characters who challenge societal norms.

In essence, Portia embodies a harmonious blend of beauty, intellect, and virtue, giving her a multifaceted appeal. Her ability to navigate her father's will, her articulate defense in court, and her successful handling of the ring trick all attest to her wisdom and astuteness. Meanwhile, her compassion, as she pleads for mercy, and her love for Bassanio highlight her emotional depth.

Portia's character serves as a catalyst, propelling the plot forward while providing moral and emotional anchors to the narrative. Her interventions lead to the resolution of the play's central conflicts, revealing her as a vital force that balances love, friendship, justice, and mercy.

In conclusion, Portia is an epitome of feminine strength and intelligence in Shakespeare's canon. Her character offers an inspiring study of a woman who navigates the constraints of her world with grace, wit, and virtue. Through Portia, Shakespeare delivers an enduring message about the strength of character and the transformative power of wisdom and love. She stands out as an iconic heroine who continues to inspire audiences with her depth, resilience, and humanity.

DESCRIBE SHYLOCK

Shylock, the Jewish moneylender in Shakespeare's "The Merchant of Venice," is a character of profound complexity and enduring controversy. His portrayal straddles the line between villain and victim, serving as a conduit for the play's exploration of themes such as justice, mercy, prejudice, and the interplay of religious and secular laws.

From his very first appearance in the play, Shylock embodies the stereotype of the avaricious moneylender, a common caricature of Jews in Elizabethan England. He justifies his practice of usury by referring to biblical precedents, which underscores his adherence to Old Testament principles: "He lends out money gratis and brings down the rate of usance here with us in Venice" (Act 1, Scene 3). This solidifies his image as a crafty, mercenary figure, an outsider in Christian Venice.

Shylock's relationship with Antonio, who personifies the Christian ethos of charity and mercy, brings the religious and cultural differences into sharp relief. Their enmity is multifaceted—rooted in religious intolerance, personal resentment, and economic rivalry. Shylock's iconic "Hath not a Jew eyes?" speech (Act 3, Scene 1) underscores his resentment against the prejudice he faces, humanizing him while revealing the play's critical examination of bigotry.

His bond with Antonio, a pound of flesh for three thousand ducats, is arguably the play's most controversial aspect. It serves as a tangible manifestation of Shylock's desire for revenge against his Christian oppressor. Despite the ghastly nature of the bond, it reflects Shylock's desperate need for validation and respect in a society that continuously demeans him. In this context, Shylock becomes a sympathetic character, a victim of societal bigotry and religious discrimination.

However, Shylock's insistence on exacting the bond, even after being offered multiple compensations, reasserts his villainous image. His refusal to show mercy in the trial scene, insisting on 'justice' instead, contrasts with Portia's renowned plea for mercy: "The quality of mercy is not strained" (Act 4, Scene 1). This stubborn pursuit of revenge even at the cost of human life casts him as a ruthless antagonist.

Yet, Shylock's tragic fall in the trial scene—where he loses his wealth and is forced to convert to Christianity—elicits a sense of sympathy. The punishment seems excessive, revealing the harshness of Venetian justice and the deep-seated prejudice against Jews.

Shylock's relationship with his daughter Jessica adds another layer to his character. Jessica's elopement with Lorenzo, a Christian, and her conversion to Christianity is a significant blow to Shylock. His anguish over her departure, tangled with his anger at the loss of his ducats, adds a familial dimension to his character, hinting at his isolation and emotional vulnerability.

It's worth noting that the interpretation of Shylock's character has evolved over time, reflecting changing societal attitudes towards anti-Semitism. During the Elizabethan era, Shylock was often depicted as a comic villain. However, later interpretations, especially post-Holocaust, have emphasized his victimhood and the anti-Semitic prejudice he faces. This interpretive flexibility attests to the richness and complexity of Shylock's character.

Shylock, despite his vengeful streak and mercenary nature, is not entirely devoid of redeeming qualities. He shows a certain resilience and intelligence in navigating a society that despises him. His adherence to his faith, in the face of prejudice and humiliation, portrays him as a character of resolve and conviction.

In conclusion, Shylock is a character of immense complexity, a blend of villainy and victimhood. He encapsulates the tension between justice and mercy, love and revenge, and religious and secular laws that pervades the play. His character serves as a mirror to the society's biases, while raising critical questions about religious tolerance, justice, and the nature of humanity. Despite the controversy surrounding his character, Shylock remains one of the most compelling and enduring characters in Shakespearean drama.

DESCRIBE JESSICA

Jessica, the daughter of Shylock in Shakespeare's "The Merchant of Venice," is a character of intrigue and considerable symbolic significance. Despite her limited presence on stage, she makes a lasting impact, serving as a bridge between the polarized worlds of Christian Venice and the Jewish ghetto, embodying themes of rebellion, religious conversion, love, and loss.

Jessica's first mention in the play paints her as a dutiful daughter, confined to the domestic sphere of her father's house: "Lock up my doors," Shylock commands, and she obeys (Act 2, Scene 5). She appears trapped, reflecting the traditional societal expectations of women during the Elizabethan era. However, beneath this veneer of compliance, Jessica harbors a deep desire for freedom and love, revealing an internal conflict that shapes her character arc.

One of the most pivotal moments in the play is Jessica's elopement with Lorenzo, a Christian. This act signifies her rebellion against her father and her Jewish heritage. She steals Shylock's ducats and precious jewels and later squanders them, adding a sense of betrayal to her rebellion: "I have a father, you a daughter, lost" (Act 2, Scene 8). This rebelliousness underscores her determination to escape her oppressive circumstances and pursue her desire for love and freedom.

Jessica's conversion to Christianity as part of her elopement is a controversial aspect of her character. Her decision signifies her assimilation into the Venetian Christian society, leaving behind her Jewish roots. Yet, her conversion is complicated. Does she willingly embrace Christianity, or is it a prerequisite to her marriage to Lorenzo? The text leaves this ambiguous, inviting various interpretations.

Her relationship with Lorenzo reveals the romantic dimension of her character. She is portrayed as a devoted lover, willing to defy societal norms and familial ties for Lorenzo's love: "I am content," she asserts, as she plans her escape (Act 2, Scene 3). Despite their love, there are moments of discord, suggesting the complexities in their relationship due to their differing cultural backgrounds. Their dialogues about love and fidelity in Act 5 provide a glimpse into their romantic dynamics and add depth to Jessica's character.

Yet, Jessica is also a character of melancholy and loss. Her decision to elope and convert results in a sense of estrangement from her past. The poignancy of her statement, "I am never merry when I hear sweet music" (Act 5, Scene 1), suggests a sense of regret and sadness, hinting at her loss of cultural identity. This emotional depth contributes to the complexity of her character.

Jessica's relationship with her father, Shylock, is central to understanding her character. Her decision to leave her father causes Shylock great distress, revealing his paternal love tangled with material loss. Yet, Jessica's reasons for leaving remain implicit. Is it her father's stern demeanor, the limitations of her Jewish identity, or simply her love for Lorenzo that drives her away? Shakespeare leaves this open to interpretation, enhancing her character's complexity.

Jessica's character serves a symbolic role in the play. Her transition from Shylock's Jewish daughter to Lorenzo's Christian wife signifies the tension and interplay between different religions and cultures in Venice. Her character embodies the exploration of identity, assimilation, and religious tolerance, themes that remain relevant today.

In conclusion, Jessica's character offers a compelling narrative of rebellion, love, conversion, and loss. She navigates the complex realities of religious and cultural divides in Venetian society, making her an intriguing figure. Despite her limited presence, she leaves a lasting impression, shedding light on the dilemmas of personal freedom, love, and identity in a deeply divided society. Through Jessica, Shakespeare explores the human capacity for love, resilience, and adaptability in the face of societal constraints.

Describe Lorenzo

Lorenzo, a Christian gentleman and friend of Antonio and Bassanio in William Shakespeare's "The Merchant of Venice," is a character defined by his romantic spirit, loyalty, and crucial role in the play's exploration of religious and cultural conflicts. Despite not being a titular character, Lorenzo's actions and relationships significantly influence the trajectory of the narrative.

At the core of Lorenzo's character is his romantic relationship with Jessica, Shylock's Jewish daughter. Lorenzo's affection for Jessica is evident from the beginning, and his intention to elope with her becomes a significant plot point. Their romance is described as passionate and consuming, as expressed in Lorenzo's words, "For she is wise, if I can judge of her, And fair she is, if that mine eyes be true" (Act 2, Scene 6). This romance symbolizes the possibility of love transcending religious and cultural barriers, lending an idealistic, romantic dimension to Lorenzo's character.

Lorenzo's character is further defined by his role in the act of elopement. He masterminds the escape plan, demonstrating a willingness to defy societal norms and risk personal safety for love. Yet, his action prompts significant consequences, including Shylock's heartbreak and subsequent insistence on exacting the flesh bond from Antonio, which form the crux of the play's conflict.

However, there's a moral ambiguity to Lorenzo's actions. His willingness to facilitate Jessica's conversion to Christianity and acceptance of Shylock's stolen wealth raise ethical questions. These actions, while justified by his love for Jessica, underscore the tension between religious affiliations and moral actions in the play.

Lorenzo's relationship with his Christian friends—Antonio and Bassanio—reveals his loyalty and camaraderie. He participates in Bassanio's venture to win Portia, supports Antonio during the trial, and even safeguards Belmont in Bassanio's absence, displaying dependability and companionship. Lorenzo's dialogue and interactions with his friends also provide comic relief and moments of introspection, enriching the narrative.

His loyalty is further exemplified when he keeps Jessica's conversion and elopement secret from his friends until it is safe, demonstrating his protective instinct. The joyous reunion with his friends after the elopement marks a turning point in the plot, highlighting Lorenzo's central role in the narrative.

As the husband of Jessica, Lorenzo navigates the complexities of an interfaith marriage. There are subtle indications of tension between them, which capture the difficulties of cultural assimilation and the persistence of prejudice. Their playful banter about unfaithful husbands and wives in Act 5 reveals their relationship's nuances, offering a deeper insight into Lorenzo's character.

Lorenzo's appreciation for music and poetry further fleshes out his character. His conversation with Jessica in Act 5 under the moonlight, accompanied by music, is one of the play's most lyrically beautiful moments. Lorenzo's assertion that "The man that hath no music in himself...is fit for treasons, stratagems, and spoils" (Act 5, Scene 1) reflects his sensitivity and aesthetic sensibilities, enriching his character.

In conclusion, Lorenzo's character, with its romantic charm, moral ambiguity, and loyal friendship, contributes significantly to the narrative and thematic depth of "The Merchant of Venice." His role in the elopement and Jessica's conversion foregrounds the play's exploration of religious intolerance, love, and the cost of freedom. Lorenzo's character embodies the idea that love can transcend societal barriers, yet it also subtly interrogates the moral complexities associated with such transgressions. His character, thus, offers a nuanced exploration of love, friendship, and religious conflict within the socio-cultural fabric of Shakespearean Venice.

Describe Gratiano

Gratiano, a character in William Shakespeare's "The Merchant of Venice," is not at the heart of the play's primary narrative, yet his personality, relationships, and role in critical scenes make him an integral part of the drama. Gratiano is a friend to Antonio and Bassanio, a companion to the protagonists, and eventually becomes Nerissa's husband. His character is typified by a boisterous nature, a sharp tongue, and a propensity for merriment and mockery, yet his growth and development throughout the play bring depth and complexity to his role.

From the onset, Gratiano is established as a garrulous and jovial individual. His speech often overflows with wit and humor, as evident in the first act when he says, "I'll hold thee any wager, When we are both accoutred like young men, I'll prove the prettier fellow of the two" (Act 1, Scene 1). His lightheartedness and flamboyance often border on excess, creating both amusement and annoyance among his companions. He often delivers comic relief in the play, breaking tension and adding levity to intense situations.

Gratiano's character is also marked by his frankness and propensity for outspoken criticism. He is vocal about his disdain for Shylock's demeanor and rigidity in enforcing the bond, as displayed in his statement, "Thou art too wild, too rude and bold of voice" (Act 1, Scene 1). His outspoken nature is a double-edged sword; while it often serves to express the audience's frustration with Shylock, it can also make Gratiano appear insensitive and brash.

His relationship with Bassanio reveals a steadfast friendship and loyalty. He accompanies Bassanio to Belmont to woo Portia and stands by Antonio during the trial. Despite his exuberant nature, he demonstrates the ability to rein in his behavior when necessary, as seen when Bassanio asks him to behave more seriously in Belmont: "Thou art too wild, too rude, and bold of voice" (Act 2, Scene 2). This shows a sense of adaptability and maturity in his character.

The romantic side of Gratiano is revealed through his relationship with Nerissa, Portia's lady-in-waiting. He woos and marries Nerissa in parallel to the primary romantic arc between Bassanio and Portia. His marriage to Nerissa, however, is not without its conflicts. The playful quarrel over the ring in the final act of the play brings comic relief but also highlights issues of trust and fidelity in their relationship.

Gratiano plays a pivotal role in the courtroom scene, which is at the heart of the play's conflict. His outbursts and harsh words for Shylock underline the hostility and tension between Christians and Jews in Venetian society: "O, be thou damned, inexecrable dog!" (Act 4, Scene 1). While his reactions may seem extreme, they reflect the larger societal prejudices and animosity at the time.

In conclusion, Gratiano's character, though not central to the plot, is a crucial element in "The Merchant of Venice." His jovial nature, outspokenness, loyalty, and romantic engagements add layers of complexity, humor, and tension to the narrative. Despite his boisterous demeanor, his capacity for loyalty and love reveal a multi-faceted character. Through Gratiano, Shakespeare explores themes of friendship, love, prejudice, and the struggle between restraint and expression in a societal setting bound by strict codes of conduct and deep-seated prejudice. His character serves as a lens to view the stark societal and cultural conflicts of the time, providing insight into the complexities of the world that shapes the play's events.

DESCRIBE NERISSA

Nerissa, one of the main female characters in Shakespeare's "The Merchant of Venice," may initially appear to be a minor character, but her role is crucial in both the narrative progression and thematic development of the play. She serves as Portia's confidante, friend, and lady-in-waiting, and is later introduced as Gratiano's love interest. While Nerissa's character is often overshadowed by the more dramatic personalities in the play, her intelligence, wit, loyalty, and moral sensibility contribute significantly to the texture of the drama.

From the outset, Nerissa's close relationship with Portia is pivotal. She provides emotional support to Portia, offering advice and companionship. This is seen in their opening exchange about the lottery of the caskets that Portia's suitors must choose from to win her hand: "Your father was ever virtuous, and holy men at their death have good inspirations" (Act 1, Scene 2). Here, Nerissa not only consoles Portia but also provides a moral perspective, revealing her wisdom and sense of justice.

Nerissa is marked by her wit and intelligence. She often mirrors Portia's intellectual acuity, showing her own sharpness of mind and capacity for clever dialogue. For example, in Act 1, Scene 2, Nerissa skillfully recalls the faults and merits of each of Portia's suitors, demonstrating her observational prowess and humor. She also plays a significant role in the execution of Portia's plan to save Antonio, showing her capability in critical situations.

Her romance with Gratiano parallels the main love story of Portia and Bassanio. Her relationship with Gratiano develops quickly and they marry soon after Bassanio wins Portia. Their relationship adds a secondary romantic thread, providing additional depth and complexity to the play's exploration of love, marriage, and loyalty. It also brings lightness and humor, contrasting the high-stakes drama of Antonio's trial.

Nerissa's loyalty to Portia is one of her defining attributes. She willingly disguises herself as a lawyer's clerk to support Portia in her plan to rescue Antonio, demonstrating her commitment and bravery. This loyalty extends to her new husband, Gratiano, even when they argue over the ring that she, disguised as the clerk, had given him: "If you had known the virtue of the ring, Or half her worthiness that gave the ring...You would not then have parted with the ring" (Act 5, Scene 1). Here, Nerissa effectively tests Gratiano's fidelity, showing her assertiveness and highlighting the theme of trust in marital relationships.

Nerissa's character also illuminates the play's exploration of class and social hierarchies. As Portia's lady-in-waiting, she represents a lower social class than the main characters. Yet, she marries Gratiano, blurring the lines of social distinction and suggesting the potential for social mobility. Her interactions with Launcelot Gobbo, who is of a lower social status, further reflect this theme.

In conclusion, Nerissa's character, though not as dramatic or dominant as others in the play, provides critical support to the narrative progression and thematic richness of "The Merchant of Venice." Her wit, loyalty, intelligence, and moral sensibility, combined with her crucial role in the narrative, make her an indispensable character. Her relationship with Portia and her marriage to Gratiano not only add layers of depth to the plot but also illuminate central themes such as loyalty, love, trust, and the fluidity of social hierarchies. Through Nerissa, Shakespeare invites us to consider the essential contributions of seemingly minor characters in shaping the outcomes of a narrative and the exploration of its themes.

Minor characters

In "The Merchant of Venice," several minor characters play critical roles that enhance the development of the plot, contribute to the main themes, and provide depth and context to the story.

1. **Launcelot Gobbo:** Launcelot is Shylock's servant who later becomes a servant to Bassanio. He adds a comedic element to the play but also provides commentary on the societal prejudices of the time. His internal debate about leaving Shylock in Act 2, Scene 2, underscores the prevailing stereotypes and biases against Shylock and Jews in general: "Certainly the Jew is the very devil incarnation" (Act 2, Scene 2). Later, Launcelot's farcical exchange with his blind father, Old Gobbo, contributes to the play's theme of misidentification and deception.

2. **Prince of Morocco and Prince of Arragon:** These two characters are suitors to Portia, and their attempts to win her hand in marriage serve to advance the plot. Their unsuccessful choices of caskets underline the theme of appearance versus reality. Both princes choose the gold and silver caskets based on their external value, which mirrors the societal obsession with wealth and status. Their failed attempts pave the way for Bassanio to succeed, underscoring the importance of inner virtue over external appearances.

3. **Salerio and Solanio:** These characters are friends of Antonio and Bassanio, and serve as narrative tools to relay information about events unfolding offstage. For instance, in Act 1, Scene 1, Solanio interprets Antonio's sadness as a worry for his ships at sea, introducing the audience to Antonio's financial stakes. Their mocking of Shylock after Jessica's elopement in Act 3, Scene 1, further emphasizes the prevalent anti-Semitism.

4. **The Duke of Venice:** The Duke presides over Antonio's trial. Though he has limited power over Shylock due to the laws that govern their contract, he clearly sympathizes with Antonio: "I am sorry for thee. Thou art come to answer A stony adversary" (Act 4, Scene 1). The Duke's position reflects the societal bias towards Christians, and his inability to intervene in the contract underscores the rigidity of the law.

5. **Tubal:** Tubal, a friend of Shylock and the only other Jewish character in the play, provides Shylock with information about Jessica. His role is limited but important as he inadvertently fuels Shylock's anger towards Antonio, further influencing the dramatic climax of the court scene.

In conclusion, even minor characters in "The Merchant of Venice" significantly influence the course of the play. They help establish the societal context, add comedic relief, and contribute to the central themes of prejudice, law, love, and the tension between appearances and reality. Their roles might be limited, but their impacts on the narrative and thematic development are substantial.

— • —

Important relationships

"The Merchant of Venice" by William Shakespeare is characterized by a web of complex relationships that drive the plot and explore key themes. The interpersonal dynamics between characters shed light on issues such as love, friendship, prejudice, religious tension, and the conflict between mercy and justice.

Antonio and Bassanio's Friendship:

The bond between Antonio, the titular merchant, and Bassanio, a young Venetian, is one of the cornerstones of the play. Bassanio is indebted to Antonio, both financially and emotionally, and Antonio's willingness to risk his life for Bassanio underscores the depth of their friendship. This relationship sets the play in motion when Antonio borrows money from Shylock to help Bassanio woo Portia: "To you, Antonio, I owe the most, in money and in love" (Act 1, Scene 1). The self-sacrificial nature of their friendship is a constant theme, highlighting the strength and potentially destructive nature of their bond.

Portia and Nerissa's Friendship:

Portia, the heiress of Belmont, and Nerissa, her lady-in-waiting, share a close relationship. Nerissa provides emotional support to Portia and serves as her confidante, helping her navigate the challenges posed by her father's will and later, Antonio's trial. Their friendship emphasizes the theme of loyalty. They also provide a contrast to the male friendships in the play, demonstrating understanding and empathy as they navigate their circumstances together: "I had rather be married to a death's-head with a bone in his mouth than to either of these" (Act 1, Scene 2).

Portia and Bassanio's Love:

The romantic relationship between Portia and Bassanio is central to the plot. Bassanio's successful choice of the lead casket wins him Portia's hand and fortune, which he uses to save Antonio. Their love, though initially overshadowed by Bassanio's financial needs, blossoms into mutual admiration and respect. Portia's intelligence and resourcefulness become apparent when she poses as Balthazar, the young lawyer, at Antonio's trial, highlighting her love for Bassanio: "They are as sick that surfeit with too much as they that starve with nothing" (Act 2, Scene 7).

Jessica and Lorenzo's Love:

Jessica, Shylock's daughter, and Lorenzo, a Christian and friend of Antonio, share a love that transcends religious boundaries. Their elopement and Jessica's subsequent conversion to Christianity intensify Shylock's animosity towards Antonio and his friends, further complicating the plot. This relationship explores the theme of religious tension and the struggle for personal freedom against societal and familial expectations: "Here, catch this casket; it is worth the pains" (Act 2, Scene 6).

Shylock and Jessica's Father-Daughter Relationship:

Shylock's relationship with his daughter, Jessica, reflects the familial tensions within the play. Jessica's elopement with Lorenzo and her theft of Shylock's ducats and precious turquoise ring deepen Shylock's resentment, leading to his insistence on claiming a pound of Antonio's flesh as agreed in their bond. This relationship underscores the themes of betrayal, religious conflict, and the tension between personal vengeance and mercy: "I would my daughter were dead at my foot, and the jewels in her ear!" (Act 3, Scene 1).

Antonio and Shylock's Rivalry:

Antonio, a Christian, and Shylock, a Jew, share a bitter rivalry. Their relationship is a study in religious intolerance, revenge, and the quest for justice. Antonio's public humiliation of Shylock and his role in influencing Shylock's customers to default on their loans fuel Shylock's desire for revenge: "He hath disgraced me, and hindered me half a million" (Act 3, Scene 1). Their enmity culminates in the trial scene where the concepts of justice and mercy are poignantly contrasted.

In conclusion, the relationships in "The Merchant of Venice" shape the plot, inform the characters' motivations, and give life to the play's themes. Through these dynamics, Shakespeare explores the complexities of love, friendship, religious tension, and the conflict between justice and mercy, creating a rich tapestry of human interactions and emotions that resonate beyond the context of the play.

Portia and Bassanio's love

Portia and Bassanio's love story serves as the romantic core of William Shakespeare's "The Merchant of Venice." Their relationship drives much of the plot and intertwines with the play's major themes, such as the distinction between appearance and reality, the power of choice, and the triumph of love over adversity.

When we first meet Bassanio, he is planning to court Portia, not purely out of love but also for financial gain: "In Belmont is a lady richly left; And she is fair, and, fairer than that word" (Act 1, Scene 1). His initial motivations to pursue Portia are largely driven by his need to settle his debts. Still, it's evident he finds her attractive and has genuine affection for her, demonstrating that his interest isn't solely mercenary.

Portia, constrained by her father's will, is bound to marry the man who correctly chooses among three caskets - gold, silver, and lead. Though initially resigned to her fate, Portia's demeanor changes upon meeting Bassanio. Her affection for him is evident when she subtly hints at the correct casket to choose: "I could teach you how to choose right, but then I am forsworn" (Act 3, Scene 2). She expresses relief when Bassanio makes the correct choice, signifying the growth of her feelings towards him.

Shakespeare takes us deeper into their relationship with Bassanio's choice of the lead casket. The inscription on the casket reads: "Who chooseth me must give and hazard all he hath." This selection reveals the depth of Bassanio's commitment to Portia. He's willing to risk everything for a chance to win her love, indicating that his affection has grown beyond the allure of her wealth. Bassanio's choice demonstrates the authenticity of his feelings and his understanding of true love's nature: "But thou, thou meagre lead, Which rather threatenest than dost promise aught...Thy paleness moves me more than eloquence" (Act 3, Scene 2).

Their bond strengthens as they overcome obstacles together. The most significant test of their love comes during the trial of Antonio, Bassanio's friend. Portia disguises herself as Balthazar, a young lawyer, and saves Antonio from Shylock's vengeance. Her intelligence and resourcefulness in this situation are revealed not only to the audience but also to Bassanio. Upon learning the truth, Bassanio's respect and love for Portia are deepened, and their relationship evolves from an initial attraction to a partnership built on mutual admiration and respect.

In Act 5, the play resolves the minor conflict between Portia and Bassanio regarding the ring he promised never to part with but did so to thank Balthazar. This subplot adds a comedic element and further tests their trust and understanding. Portia, in the end, reveals that she was the lawyer, and the playful deception concludes with shared laughter, reinforcing their bond: "Pardon this fault, and by my soul I swear I never more will break an oath with thee" (Act 5, Scene 1).

Throughout the play, the love between Portia and Bassanio matures and evolves. From Bassanio's initial pursuit of wealth and status, it transitions into a mutual admiration and deep respect, solidified by their shared experiences and trials. Their relationship is a testament to the power of love to transcend initial intentions and evolve into something genuine and profound.

In conclusion, Portia and Bassanio's love story represents a journey of growth, understanding, and mutual respect. It intertwines with the central themes of the play and drives much of the plot. Through their relationship, Shakespeare explores the transformative power of love and its ability to bring out the best in people, providing a touching and nuanced romantic subplot to the broader narrative of "The Merchant of Venice."

JESSICA AND LORENZO'S LOVE

Jessica and Lorenzo's relationship in William Shakespeare's "The Merchant of Venice" provides a contrasting subplot to the main narrative. Their love is one that defies societal expectations and religious boundaries, representing a form of rebellion against the entrenched norms of their time.

Jessica, Shylock's daughter, finds herself stifled under her father's oppressive rule. Lorenzo, a friend of Bassanio, is a Christian, making their love both a social and religious transgression in the context of Venetian society. Their relationship underscores the play's themes of religious conflict, personal freedom, and the struggle to reconcile identity with love.

The couple's first action is a daring one: Jessica decides to elope with Lorenzo. This step is a rebellion against her father's strict control and the religious barrier separating them: "I am much ashamed of my exchange: But love is blind, and lovers cannot see" (Act 2, Scene 6). To do this, Jessica disguises herself as a page boy, a symbol of her desire to escape her current identity and a further demonstration of the theme of appearance versus reality.

Jessica's conversion to Christianity for Lorenzo symbolizes her commitment to their relationship and her personal freedom. Still, it complicates her relationship with her father and reinforces the play's exploration of religious tension: "I shall be saved by my husband. He hath made me a Christian" (Act 3, Scene 5). The conversion, though a symbol of her devotion to Lorenzo, becomes a point of contention with Shylock, who feels betrayed and victimized, escalating the antagonism between him and the Christian community.

The elopement is a daring act, both for Jessica, who steals her father's ducats and a precious turquoise ring, and Lorenzo, who risks the wrath of a powerful moneylender. Their willingness to risk societal ostracism and Shylock's vengeance reveals their love's depth and strength.

Throughout the play, Jessica struggles with guilt over her actions and her identity as a Jew. Despite her love for Lorenzo, she expresses remorse for betraying her father and abandoning her faith: "I am never merry when I hear sweet music" (Act 5, Scene 1). Yet, despite these struggles, her relationship with Lorenzo remains solid, further underscoring their love's resilience.

Lorenzo, for his part, is a consistent source of support for Jessica. He reassures her of her new place in Christian society, tries to ease her guilt over her actions, and openly expresses his love for her. His defense of Jessica during their moonlit exchange in Act 5, Scene 1 further solidifies their bond and validates their decision to be together despite the societal barriers they had to overcome.

However, their relationship isn't without its trials. In Act 3, Scene 5, Lorenzo humorously chides Jessica about her prodigality, hinting at future conflicts and their differing upbringings and worldviews. Nevertheless, their love, strengthened by their shared experiences and struggles, allows them to navigate these potential obstacles.

In conclusion, Jessica and Lorenzo's love story in "The Merchant of Venice" is a tale of daring, sacrifice, and resilience. It provides an exploration of the conflict between personal desire and societal expectations, the struggle for identity, and the power of love to transcend boundaries. Through their relationship, Shakespeare explores the complexities and consequences of love in a world divided by religious tension and social norms.

SHYLOCK AND JESSICA'S FATHER-DAUGHTER RELATIONSHIP

The father-daughter relationship between Shylock and Jessica in "The Merchant of Venice" is complex, embodying the tension of their differing worldviews and the societal context in which they exist. Through their relationship, Shakespeare explores themes of familial duty, personal freedom, cultural identity, and the lasting impact of intolerance and prejudice.

Shylock is depicted as a stern and controlling father, placing stringent restrictions on Jessica's social life. His strict observance of Jewish customs and his suspicion of Christians confine Jessica to their home: "Lock up my doors; and when you hear the drum...Do not thrust your head into the public street" (Act 2, Scene 5). His overbearing demeanor stems from his desire to protect Jessica from a society that holds prejudice against their faith.

At the same time, Shylock's avaricious nature often overshadows his paternal affection. His wealth becomes a divisive element in their relationship. When Jessica elopes with Lorenzo, a Christian, and steals his money and jewels, Shylock's outrage centers as much on his lost wealth as on his daughter's betrayal: "My daughter! O my ducats! O my daughter!" (Act 2, Scene 8). This emphasis on material loss over personal betrayal paints Shylock as a materialistic father, undermining the sympathy the audience might have felt for his plight.

Jessica, on the other hand, feels stifled under her father's rule. Her rebellious spirit is evident in her decision to elope with Lorenzo, an act of defiance that underscores her desire for personal freedom. Jessica's actions reflect a struggle common to many young adults - the yearning for independence and the need to define one's own identity.

Yet, Jessica's elopement is a drastic step beyond mere rebellion. Her decision to convert to Christianity is a rejection of her father's faith and a painful betrayal for Shylock, who feels his own flesh and blood has turned against him: "I would my daughter were dead at my foot, and the jewels in her ear!" (Act 3, Scene 1). For Jessica, however, it's a declaration of her autonomy and a desperate attempt to fit into a society where her Jewish identity is scorned.

The repercussions of Jessica's elopement reveal a less examined facet of Shylock's character - a grieving father. His lament, "I have a daughter—Would any of the tribe of Barrabas had been her husband rather than a Christian!" (Act 3, Scene 1), is a heartfelt expression of loss and betrayal. Despite his anger, there is an underlying sadness, suggesting a profound sense of paternal love that could have been overshadowed by his avarice and rigid ways.

The estrangement between Jessica and Shylock also reflects the broader religious and cultural divide in Venetian society. Their relationship becomes a casualty of societal prejudice and Jessica's desire to escape it, offering a critique of the harmful impact of societal divisions on personal relationships.

In conclusion, the relationship between Shylock and Jessica in "The Merchant of Venice" is a complex interplay of familial affection, personal freedom, cultural identity, and societal prejudice. Through their relationship, Shakespeare highlights the consequences of intolerance and the struggles of individuals navigating societal norms to establish their identities. Despite its complexities, their relationship humanizes Shylock and provides Jessica with a narrative arc that explores the themes of rebellion, freedom, and the cost of cultural assimilation.

─ · ─

ANTONIO AND SHYLOCK'S RIVALRY

The rivalry between Antonio and Shylock is one of the most pivotal elements in Shakespeare's "The Merchant of Venice." Their relationship, characterized by deep-seated animosity, is shaped by personal resentment, religious conflict, and economic competition, forming a microcosm of the larger societal tensions in Venetian society.

From the outset, it is clear that Antonio, a successful Christian merchant, and Shylock, a Jewish moneylender, inhabit opposite ends of the societal and religious spectrum. Their professional rivalry is rooted in their differing views on money lending. Antonio lends money without interest, which undermines Shylock's business. For Shylock, Antonio's acts are not just an economic threat but an affront to his livelihood and dignity.

Religious differences further fuel their animosity. Antonio openly disparages Shylock's Jewish faith: "I am as like to call thee so again, To spit on thee again, to spurn thee too" (Act 1, Scene 3). Shylock, in turn, resents Antonio and the Christian community's religious intolerance and hypocrisy: "He hath disgraced me...laughed at my losses...thwarted my bargains...heated mine enemies; and what's his reason? I am a Jew" (Act 3, Scene 1). Their personal rivalry becomes a reflection of the religious tension permeating Venetian society.

The crux of their rivalry, however, lies in the bond of the "pound of flesh." In lending Antonio money, Shylock cleverly devises this bond, foreseeing an opportunity for retribution should Antonio default. The bond is a manifestation of Shylock's pent-up resentment, symbolizing his desire for justice: "If you repay me not on such a day, In such a place, such sum or sums as are Express'd in the condition, let the forfeit Be nominated for an equal pound Of your fair flesh..." (Act 1, Scene 3).

When Antonio's ships are reportedly lost at sea, Shylock becomes adamant about exacting his pound of flesh, pushing their rivalry to its zenith. The ensuing courtroom scene (Act 4, Scene 1) underscores their animosity, while highlighting the themes of mercy and justice. Antonio's acceptance of his fate signifies his stoicism and perceived moral superiority, while Shylock's insistence on the bond exposes his thirst for vengeance.

However, Shylock's pursuit of revenge ultimately leads to his downfall. When Portia, disguised as a lawyer, rules that Shylock can take his pound of flesh but not spill a drop of Christian blood, Shylock is left defenseless. Antonio, showing some measure of mercy, spares Shylock's life but demands he convert to Christianity and leave his wealth to Lorenzo and Jessica upon his death. This twist of fate intensifies the personal and religious conflict between them, symbolizing the victory of Christian mercy over Jewish law.

In conclusion, the rivalry between Antonio and Shylock in "The Merchant of Venice" is a complex, multilayered conflict that encapsulates the societal, religious, and economic tensions of their time. Their relationship serves as a critique of religious intolerance, the pitfalls of revenge, and the struggle for justice in a biased society. While their rivalry fuels the drama of the play, it also opens a window into the complex dynamics of power, prejudice, and identity in Shakespearean Venice.

CONFLICTS

"The Merchant of Venice" is an intricate web of conflicts that span personal, religious, societal, and moral dimensions. These conflicts serve as the driving force behind the narrative, shape character dynamics, and provide a platform for Shakespeare to explore deeper themes of love, justice, prejudice, and the human condition.

At the heart of the play is the personal conflict between Antonio, a wealthy Christian merchant, and Shylock, a Jewish moneylender. Their rivalry encapsulates a multitude of tensions, primarily stemming from their religious differences and economic competition. Antonio openly scorns Shylock for his faith and practice of usury, while Shylock harbors deep resentment against Antonio for his religious intolerance and for undermining his business. This personal vendetta culminates in the courtroom scene, where Shylock seeks to exact revenge through a "pound of flesh," pushing their rivalry to its climax.

Parallel to this is the societal conflict of Christian versus Jew. This overarching conflict permeates all aspects of the narrative, mirroring the religious intolerance of 16th-century Venice. Shylock, as a Jew, is a marginalized figure in Christian Venice, often subjected to open scorn and prejudice. His insistence on the "pound of flesh" becomes a symbol of his demand for justice and equality, starkly highlighting the societal conflict.

Another central conflict revolves around the theme of love and friendship. Bassanio's quest for Portia's hand, despite his lack of wealth, sets up the romantic conflict of the play. His reliance on Antonio's financial aid out of friendship introduces a moral dilemma when Antonio's life is put at risk due to the defaulted loan. Bassanio is torn between his love for Portia and his loyalty to Antonio, underscoring the tension between romantic love and platonic friendship.

In the realm of love, there's also Jessica and Lorenzo's elopement, which sparks the familial conflict between Jessica and her father, Shylock. Jessica's rebellion and conversion to Christianity deepen Shylock's sense of betrayal and fuel his demand for justice, amplifying the personal, religious, and familial conflicts in the play.

Portia's predicament forms another significant conflict. Bound by her father's will to marry the man who chooses the correct casket, Portia grapples with the constraints on her freedom and her growing affection for Bassanio. Her ability to navigate this conflict, eventually leading to her marriage to Bassanio, reveals her character's ingenuity and resilience.

Furthermore, the play brings to light the moral conflict between mercy and justice. This is best embodied in the trial scene where Shylock, representing strict adherence to law and justice, is countered by Portia's plea for mercy: "The quality of mercy is not strained..." (Act 4, Scene 1). The outcome of the trial raises questions about the true nature of justice and the power of mercy, leaving the audience to grapple with this moral conflict.

Lastly, there is an underlying conflict between appearance and reality that threads through the play. From Portia's disguise as a male lawyer to the deceptive appearance of the lead casket, and the seeming loyalty of Shylock's servant Launcelot, the play continuously explores the disparity between how things appear and their true nature.

In conclusion, "The Merchant of Venice" presents a complex tapestry of conflicts, each intertwining with the others to advance the narrative and deepen its thematic exploration. Whether personal, societal, religious, or moral, these conflicts serve as a reflection of the tumultuous social fabric of

Shakespearean Venice and offer a profound commentary on human nature and societal norms.

— · —

CLIMAX

"The Merchant of Venice," penned by William Shakespeare, unfolds a multitude of narrative threads, each adding depth and complexity to the plot. Yet, among these narratives, the storyline that stands out for its intensity and emotional resonance culminates in the courtroom scene (Act 4, Scene 1). It's widely recognized as the climax of the play, the crux upon which the resolution pivots.

The courtroom scene is the climactic culmination of multiple story arcs. Shylock, the beleaguered Jewish moneylender, seeks to claim a pound of flesh from Antonio, the eponymous Merchant of Venice, as repayment for a defaulted loan. Antonio's life hangs in the balance, subject to the verdict of the Duke's court. Simultaneously, Bassanio, Antonio's dear friend and the recipient of the loan that caused Antonio's predicament, is racked with guilt and anxiety. Meanwhile, unbeknownst to everyone in the court, Portia and Nerissa, the leading women of the play, assume the roles of a learned young doctor of laws and his clerk, respectively.

From the outset, this scene is characterized by high stakes and intense emotions. Shylock, who has been vilified and persecuted because of his faith, sees an opportunity to exact a measure of revenge upon Antonio, the man who embodies the Christian community's disdain for him. His single-minded determination for justice is reflected in his stubborn refusal to show mercy, ignoring pleas from the Duke and others: "I'll have my bond; speak not against my bond. I have sworn an oath that I will have my bond" (Act 4, Scene 1).

Contrarily, Antonio seems resigned to his fate, willingly prepared to give his life to honor the bond and save Bassanio from further guilt: "I am a tainted wether of the flock, Meetest for death; the weakest kind of fruit Drops earliest to the ground, and so let me" (Act 4, Scene 1).

In this context, the arrival of Portia, disguised as Balthazar, injects an undercurrent of dramatic irony into the scene. The audience, privy to her true identity, is left in anticipation of the role she's destined to play in this high-stakes scenario.

Portia's eloquent plea for mercy, while apparently going unnoticed by Shylock, sets the tone for the coming resolution: "The quality of mercy is not strain'd, It droppeth as the gentle rain from heaven Upon the place beneath" (Act 4, Scene 1). It's a pivotal moment that underscores one of the central themes of the play - the dichotomy of justice and mercy.

The climax is reached when, after initially appearing to favor Shylock's claim, Portia unveils a loophole in the bond that saves Antonio's life. In one of the play's most dramatic twists, she notes that while the bond allows Shylock to cut Antonio's flesh, it does not permit the shedding of any blood: "This bond doth give thee here no jot of blood; The words expressly are 'a pound of flesh'" (Act 4, Scene 1).

This clever manipulation of law by Portia completely reverses the situation, saving Antonio and leading to Shylock's downfall. The tension of the scene deflates rapidly from this point, and the direction of the plot changes, transitioning from rising action to falling action.

In conclusion, the courtroom scene in Act 4, Scene 1 serves as the climactic center of "The Merchant of Venice." It's a potent distillation of the play's main themes - justice, mercy, prejudice, the role of law, and the power of wit and intelligence. Its resolution not only affects the fates of the characters but also triggers contemplation about the nature of justice and mercy, making it a lasting reminder of the timeless relevance of Shakespeare's works.

Resolution

In the winding narrative that is "The Merchant of Venice," the resolution unfolds primarily across Acts 4 and 5, following the tension-filled climax of the courtroom scene. This period of resolution or denouement brings closure to the characters' intertwined stories, revealing the aftermath of the central conflict and presenting a final exploration of the play's themes.

The resolution commences in the latter part of Act 4, Scene 1, when Shylock, cornered by Portia's legal acumen, is left without his claim to Antonio's flesh. The sudden turn of events is a dramatic shift, completely reversing Shylock's fortune. He finds himself at the mercy of the court he hoped to use as a tool of revenge. Portia, continuing her legal argument, declares that Shylock has conspired against the life of a Venetian citizen. The tables have turned - now it is Shylock's life hanging in the balance: "It is enacted in the laws of Venice, if it be proved against an alien that by direct or indirect attempts he seek the life of any citizen" (Act 4, Scene 1).

Portia and the Duke show mercy, sparing Shylock's life but imposing a fine and requiring him to convert to Christianity and bequeath all his goods to Jessica and Lorenzo upon his death. Here, the play grapples with the themes of mercy, justice, and religious tolerance. Shylock, the aggrieved party, is rendered an object of mercy while being subjected to forced religious conversion, underscoring the harshness and prejudice he faces. This moment further exposes the societal and religious conflicts prevalent in Venice.

The transition to Act 4, Scene 2, is brief but essential, as it wraps up the subplot involving Portia and Nerissa's disguises. The two women cleverly obtain rings from their husbands, setting the stage for the final act's humorous revelations and reconciliations.

Act 5 serves as an extended resolution, providing a stark contrast to the intense climax of Act 4. Set in the romantic moonlight of Belmont, it is filled with the joyous reunion of lovers and friends, light banter, and lyrical poetry. Jessica and Lorenzo, now rightful heirs to Shylock's wealth, revel in their love, while Launcelot humorously debates with Jessica about her salvation. Here, the themes of love, friendship, and the quest for happiness come to the fore, offering a lighter conclusion.

When Portia and Nerissa return to Belmont, they are joyously reunited with their husbands, Bassanio and Gratiano. However, the playful quarrel about the rings adds an element of tension. Bassanio and Gratiano, not recognizing their wives as the legal professionals from the courtroom, are put to the test about their loyalty. The resolution reaches its zenith when Portia and Nerissa reveal their disguises, leaving their husbands both relieved and chastened. This instance reinforces the theme of appearance vs reality, a central motif throughout the play.

The resolution concludes with Antonio receiving good news about his previously lost ships. This welcome surprise, coupled with Shylock's downfall, suggests a shift in fortune favoring Antonio. Moreover, Portia's successful ruse, Jessica and Lorenzo's happy union, and the promise of a peaceful life ahead for the couples offer a hopeful outlook, reinforcing the comedic structure of the play.

In conclusion, the resolution of "The Merchant of Venice" offers a complex mix of joy, relief, and contemplation. While it provides closure to the play's intricate web of conflicts, it also leaves audiences grappling with deeper questions about justice, mercy, prejudice, and the power of love and friendship. These elements elevate the resolution from a simple plot device to a meaningful exploration of human values and societal norms, demonstrating the enduring relevance of Shakespeare's work.

— · —

MORAL OF THIS PLAY

"The Merchant of Venice" is a complex, multilayered play that engages with a variety of themes such as justice, mercy, the nature of love and friendship, prejudice and discrimination, and the tension between religious law and secular authority. Each of these themes carries within them several moral implications, making it hard to pin down a singular "moral of the story." However, by exploring these themes, we can identify some key moral lessons that the play offers.

1. **The Value of Mercy over Strict Justice**: One of the most memorable moments in the play is Portia's eloquent plea for mercy in Act 4, Scene 1. Arguing that "The quality of mercy is not strain'd, it droppeth as the gentle rain from heaven upon the place beneath" (4.1), she emphasizes that mercy is a divine attribute that both blesses the one who gives it and the one who receives it. In contrast, Shylock's unwavering demand for justice without mercy leads to his downfall. Thus, one moral lesson from the play is the importance of tempering justice with mercy and understanding.

2. **The Destructive Power of Hatred and Revenge**: Shylock's desire for revenge against Antonio consumes him and ultimately leads to his ruin. The play suggests that hatred and a thirst for vengeance are destructive and self-defeating. Shylock's insistence on "a pound of flesh" not only isolates him from the community but also results in him losing his wealth and being forcibly con-

verted to Christianity. This is a cautionary tale about the negative consequences of allowing oneself to be driven by resentment and revenge.

3. **The Impermanence and Deceptiveness of Material Wealth**: The play contrasts material wealth with the richness of human relationships. Antonio, though potentially ruined financially, has friends willing to risk everything for him, while Shylock, despite his wealth, is friendless and alone. Moreover, the three caskets test highlights the deceptive nature of appearances and the vanity of worldly wealth. The suitor who chooses the gold casket, which represents material wealth, is rejected, while the suitor who chooses the lead casket, which symbolizes humility and inner worth, wins Portia's hand. This suggests the moral lesson that true value is found not in external wealth but in the quality of our character and our relationships with others.

4. **The Importance of Love and Friendship**: Love and friendship are portrayed as the highest values in the play. Antonio's willingness to risk his life for Bassanio, and Portia's decision to leave Belmont and disguise herself to save Antonio, underscore the strength of their bonds of friendship and love. The friendship between Antonio and Bassanio, the romantic love between Portia and Bassanio, and even the complicated love between Jessica and Lorenzo, all demonstrate the transformative power of love and friendship. These relationships remind us of the importance of loyalty, self-sacrifice, and mutual care in human relationships.

5. **The Damaging Effects of Prejudice and Discrimination**: The play also shines a spotlight on the harm caused by religious and racial discrimination. Shylock's hatred for Antonio is partly fueled by the anti-Semitic treatment he has received from the Christian

community. His mistreatment raises moral questions about prejudice, bigotry, and the ways societies exclude or marginalize "the other." It serves as a critique of religious intolerance and a call for understanding and acceptance of diversity.

In conclusion, while "The Merchant of Venice" cannot be reduced to a single moral, it offers several moral lessons that continue to resonate in contemporary society. It prompts us to reflect on the nature of justice, the importance of mercy, the destructive power of hatred and revenge, the true value of wealth, the richness of human relationships, and the effects of prejudice and discrimination. Through these themes, the play invites us to consider what it means to be human, to live in a diverse society, and to treat each other with justice, compassion, and understanding.

— • —

Famous lines from the play

"The Merchant of Venice," one of William Shakespeare's most celebrated and frequently performed plays, is filled with memorable lines that echo with wisdom, wit, and insight. Spanning a wide range of themes such as love, mercy, justice, friendship, prejudice, and more, these lines provide a succinct, eloquent articulation of the play's main themes and character's motives. Given the rich tapestry of Shakespeare's writing, these most famous lines can only skim the surface, but it provides an opportunity to delve into the deeper meanings and implications of Shakespeare's words.

"All that glisters is not gold." (Act 2, Scene 7)

Perhaps one of the most oft-quoted lines from the play, Prince of Morocco, reads these words inscribed on a scroll within the golden casket he has chosen in his bid to win Portia's hand. This phrase has since become a proverbial warning that not everything which looks precious or true turns out to be so. In the context of the play, it speaks to the recurring theme of appearance versus reality. In the broader societal context, it warns against superficiality, urging us to look beyond outward appearances to find the true value that lies beneath.

"The quality of mercy is not strained; It droppeth as the gentle rain from heaven upon the place beneath." (Act 4, Scene 1)

This profound statement comes from Portia, who is disguised as a lawyer, as she pleads with Shylock to show mercy towards Antonio. Portia's speech on mercy is arguably the moral center of the play. She suggests that mercy is a divine attribute and should be freely given, an idea that challenges the strict adherence to the law demonstrated by Shylock. This quote is timeless and universal, conveying a moral lesson that is as relevant today as it was in Shakespeare's time.

"I am a Jew. Hath not a Jew eyes? Hath not a Jew hands, organs, dimensions, senses, affections, passions?" (Act 3, Scene 1)

Shylock's powerful speech is an indictment of the racial and religious prejudice he endures. It is an appeal to common humanity, reminding the Christian majority that Jews are human beings with the same physical and emotional experiences. Shylock demands empathy, reminding the audience that prejudice is a failure of imagination, a refusal to acknowledge common humanity.

"In sooth, I know not why I am so sad." (Act 1, Scene 1)

These opening lines of Antonio speak to the melancholic mood that permeates much of the play. It reveals Antonio's introspective nature and foreshadows the trials he will undergo. The line's enduring resonance lies in its evocation of the human experience of inexplicable sorrow, something many can relate to.

"I hold the world but as the world, Gratiano; A stage where every man must play a part, And mine a sad one." (Act 1, Scene 1)

This line, spoken by Antonio to Gratiano, hints at Shakespeare's larger theme of the world as a stage, a concept he would later expand upon in "As You Like It." Antonio's world-weariness is palpable in this line, but it also speaks to the universal human condition - the roles we are compelled to play in the grand drama of life.

"But love is blind, and lovers cannot see the pretty follies that themselves commit." (Act 2, Scene 6)

Spoken by Jessica as she elopes with Lorenzo, this line encapsulates the idea that love often overlooks faults. It's a poignant reflection on the nature of love, its blindness, its follies, and its capacity for forgiveness.

"You see me, Lord Bassanio, where I stand, Such as I am." (Act 3, Scene 2)

In this line, Portia, while asserting her position, also shows vulnerability, submitting herself to Bassanio's judgment. It exemplifies the complexities of love and the human condition's paradoxical elements – strength and vulnerability, certainty and risk, power and surrender.

In conclusion, these lines, among others, are not only memorable for their poetic quality but also for the profound truths they convey. They encapsulate the enduring relevance of "The Merchant of Venice," showing why it continues to be studied and appreciated centuries after its first performance. These lines offer timeless insights into human nature and societal values, reinforcing the play's status as a masterpiece of English literature.

www.ingramcontent.com/pod-product-compliance
Lightning Source LLC
Chambersburg PA
CBHW071204120626
46546CB00006B/2405